48 Decidedly Different Creative Writing Prompts

Aligns to NCTE Standards

**Mark H. Larson and
Robert S. Boone**

A GOOD YEAR BOOK™

Good Year Books
Tucson, Arizona

Dedication

To the memory of Professor Wallace W. Douglas of Northwestern University: "The mind boggles."

Good Year Books

Our titles are available for most basic curriculum subjects plus many enrichment areas. For more Good Year Books, contact your local bookseller or educational dealer. For a complete catalog with information about other Good Year Books, please contact:

Good Year Books
PO Box 91858
Tucson, AZ 85752-1858
www.goodyearbooks.com

Library of Congress Catloging-in-Publication Data
Larson, Mark.
 Moe's café : 48 decidedly different creative writing
 prompts / Mark H. Larson, Robert S. Boone.
 p. cm.
 ISBN-13: 978-1-59647-088-0
 ISBN-10: 1-59647-088-7
 1. English language--Compostion and exercises--
 Study and teaching (Middle school)--United States.
 2. Creative writing (Middle School)--United States.
 I. Boone, Robert S. II. Title.

 LB1631.L263 2006
 808'.040712--dc22

                              2006043473

NCTE Standards

Moe's Café: 48 Decidedly Different Creative Writing Prompts contains lessons and activities that reinforce and develop skills as defined by the National Council of Teachers of English as appropriate for students in grades 6 to 12. These activities meet the NCTE standards regarding literary range, periods/genres, textual analysis, voice, audience, form/technique, research, technology, diversity, and purpose. See www.goodyearbooks.com for information on how specific lessons correlate to specific standards.

Cover Design: Gary D. Smith, Peformance Design
Text Design: Doug Goewey
Cover photo: 300dpiGuy, courtesy iStock.com
Interior photos:
page 3 — 300dpiGuy, courtesy iStock.com
page 53 — Nancy Louie, courtesy iStock.com
page 103 — Christine Balderas, courtesy iStock.com

It All Started with Moe . . .

ABOUT TWENTY YEARS AGO I was teaching a creative writing workshop to a group of ninth graders from Chicago's South Side. On this first meeting of a four-session program, the students were to describe a real or imaginary place. I told them to select a "memorable" place and make the readers feel they were there. I told them to follow a plan and to pack in plenty of details. I even read a few examples from former students. Description, I told the group, is something all writers need to master!

They all nodded but not agreeably. In fact, you might say that they nodded disagreeably. Instead of smiling, they scowled. Instead of sitting up eagerly, they slumped. Instead of asking me pertinent questions, they grumbled. Even the teacher who had arranged for this workshop sat in the back with a John Grisham novel nestled in her lap and yawned. This was not going to be pretty.

What to do? Should I push forward even though prospects did not look good, or should I try this new idea I had been fiddling with? I looked over as the teacher was picking up her novel and made the choice. What's there to lose?, I thought. Let's see what happens.

OK, I told the group, change of plan. Imagine that you're inside a horrible restaurant called "Moe's Café." I'm going to ask you a dozen questions. You'll scribble down quick answers. When I'm done asking, you'll take your answers and shape them into your description.

Before they had a chance to complain, I began firing off questions: *What's on the floor? How about the menu? What do you see on the wall? Name several bad smells. Where's Moe standing? What's he look like? What about that dog sleeping in the corner? How about the family that sat down next to you?* By now they were sitting up and smiling, and I could tell I was on to something. When they told me to slow down, I sped up and asked more questions: *How about Blanche the waitress? What can you tell me about the ceiling?*

Before long I was done asking questions, and they were about to begin composing. I told them that they should write this description as a letter to a friend and that they could change the order of details or add some more. Then I shut up and let them write. For an hour they were bent over, feverishly carving out their descriptions while I sat on the desk and marveled. Even the yawning teacher had put down John Grisham and was scribbling away.

When they were done, they read aloud and the results were gruesomely spectacular. One girl talked about a dead fly on the menu. Another girl described the barefoot waitress's big toe. A boy added a contrasting detail: an old lady in a white dress carefully nibbling a sandwich at a corner table. Each description was powerful in its own way. Most were funny, but a few were quite sad.

Moe's Café was born.

Over the next three sessions, I continued with the Moe Method: I put the students into a place; I asked a lot of questions. They listened, scribbled, and composed. In Session Two, they described a cozy cabin. In Session Three it was a spooky office. Session Four was a barn with a cat about to do in a mouse. On my last day, I suggested to the regular teacher that she might want to continue doing this. She said that she had already started a list, thank you. As I asked the class to think about their recent writing, I pointed out that although I may have been the one who asked the questions, they were the ones who did the actual writing, and it was very good. From now on when you write, I urged them, ask your own questions.

Through the years I have continued to teach writing workshops all over the Chicago area and have founded a program for city kids who like to write. In all of these efforts, Moe and his despicable dump have been at my side. No matter whom or where I taught, I would always ask my writers to stop in first at Moe's Café.

Now fellow Moe's regular Mark Larson and I have put together a book of writing ideas inspired by Moe's Café. The prompts are varied: Some require imagination; others require memory. They all, however, involve a heavy dose of questions and answers. As Moe himself might have said, "You ain't going to write something until you have something to write. Hot cap on that coffee?"

Bob Boone
Founder,
Young Chicago Authors

Mark Henry Larson
Northwestern University
Center for Talent Development

Contents

Introduction

To the Teacher

We are excited about this book for many reasons, not the least of which is that we are anxious to use it ourselves with our own students. Although designed to be used as the primary text for a creative writing course, the book can be easily adapted for use as a component to a general English course, as a guide for a creative writing club, or as a workbook for a self-directed or tutored individual.

The two biggest strengths of this book are its effectiveness and its versatility. We know that both this method and these exercises work because we have used them ourselves in a number of diverse settings within and beyond the traditional classroom. They have worked with pre-teens, teens, and adults. They have worked with highly motivated college-bound kids, with "at-risk" students placed in alternate school settings, with adults in writing workshops, with individual students working online, and with creative writing clubs.

Because the forty-eight prompts do not necessarily need to be taught in sequence, you can feel free to pick and choose those that appeal to you and your students. Most of the activities can be done with or without a teacher's presence, and the balance can be adjusted between in-class work and homework assignments as the teacher sees fit. This makes them especially useful for those times when you wish to conference with individuals or on those days when a substitute teacher is handling your class. A possible weekly sequence could be set up as follows:

Monday: Read prompt (Start). Answer ten questions (Questions). Organize material (Getting Ready). Share results. Homework: Write mini-stories (Starting Your Story).

Tuesday: Share mini-stories. Homework: Read suggested short story (Read and Write).

Wednesday: Discuss short story. Begin drafting (Write Away). Homework: First draft (Write Away!).

Thursday: Peer edit drafts. View and discuss film scene (On the Screen). Homework: Revise draft.

Friday: Share and discuss drafts.

Although the lessons do work by themselves—we use a number of them "as is" for our online creative writing course—they are more fun and effective when you yourself become involved in the question process. This provides you with an opportunity to branch off and supplement these questions with more of your own—especially as your students become more excited about their creations.

Each lesson also contains suggestions for short stories and film scenes that are closely connected to the story prompts. In a creative writing course, these may be used as writing models and discussion starters for the individual prompts. These same story and film suggestions could form the curriculum of a short story and/or film study unit or component in a general English foundations course. Most of the short story selections are gleaned from commonly found school anthologies and/or accessible online short story sites. Keeping in mind the legal restrictions of showing certain films in the classroom, we have only included films that are rated G, PG, or PG-13 in our film selections. Though the films could be viewed in their entirety, specific scenes have been earmarked for analysis so that the exercise need not use up more class time than you can afford.

Good luck and welcome to Moe's—the pie is great, but watch out for the chili.

To the Young Prose Writer

There are several possible reasons why you may now own this book. Maybe you are taking a creative writing course and you had to buy it. Perhaps you are intrigued by the short story form and want to try your hand at writing some Poe-like thrillers, science fiction adventures, or social reality scenarios on your own. You may even be a creative writer already and want to continue something you already have going.

In any case, you must have decided that creative writing matters, that it is something you want to do well. Maybe you want to be a writer, or maybe you just want to find out if you want to be a writer. Maybe you are a different kind of writer, but you think creative writing will help you develop other skills.

Although creative writing shares many similarities with other types of writing, it does differ in some important respects from most of the writing done in schools. In English class, you frequently write about literature: You make statements, which you then prove by citing examples from your reading or research. Your work is evaluated according to how clearly, convincingly, and correctly you make your point.

With creative writing, however, instead of analyzing poems or stories, you actually write the poems and stories yourself. Your material comes from your imagination and memory. Instead of being as clear and direct as possible, you try to be more subtle and indirect. In some cases, *how* you write will be more important than *what* you write. Instead of appealing to your readers' sense of logic, you must also appeal to their feelings. You expect more of your audience.

Like most creative writing books, this one has many prompts to help you to get started. Unlike the prompts in most other books, though, these prompts include lots of questions for you to answer before you get started. These questions are designed to help you think deeply and creatively about your subject beforehand. Once you have answered these questions, you should be ready and anxious to write.

Another unique feature of the "Moe method" is the "mini-story" approach. After the questions have helped you to think a bit about a particular story, you will write several ninety-word mini-stories. These mini-stories are either basic plot summaries or short excerpts of possible full-length versions of your story. By experimenting with these very short versions, you will quickly get an idea of what story approach will work best for you. Most writers do some sort of trial-and-error method like this before they decide on how to approach their stories. Imagine a group of television or film writers kicking around ideas for a possible new television pilot or movie: *"There's this poor artist and this beautiful girl that love each other, but her mom wants her to marry this rich jerk. They could both be on the* Titanic *and she has to sneak away. . . ."* The method is fast, fun, and effective.

In addition, each prompt suggests a short story to read and a film scene to watch that bear a close connection in theme, situation, character, or style to the story that you are writing. Each story and film suggestion includes specific advice to help you concentrate on the piece as a writer. By examining these stories and scenes, you will have a chance to compare your own work with that of professionals who have taken on similar writing challenges. Along with these professional models, the book also includes several completed short stories written by writers your age. These stories were written in response to the same prompts found in the book and provide further ideas for what makes for a successful story.

Before you get started writing, it is important to establish the basic definition of a short story and the terms associated with it. First, a familiarity with these literary terms will provide a common vocabulary for

describing the elements that should be included within your story. Next, these same elements will provide a basic framework for the critical questions you will ask yourself as you go back to improve your work.

The short story is a relatively short piece of *prose* fiction, narrated from a single *point of view* and taking place in a distinctive *setting*. It has a series of actions or *plot* built around a central issue or *conflict*. Usually this involves at least one *character* whose life may be significantly changed once the issue is resolved. The *tone* of a short story can be funny or serious, realistic or fantastic, straightforward or satiric. The story can be strictly entertaining or much more *thematic*.

The following questions will first serve as a *descriptive* guide as to what should be included within your story, then afterward they will serve as a *critical* guide as to what to consider in your revision process:

Point of View
- Is the right person telling the story?

Setting
- Does the story start where it should?
- Is the conflict clear?
- Does it build to a climax?
- Is there suspense?
- Does the conflict resolve itself?
- Does it end where it should?

Characters
- Are the characters well developed?
- Are they motivated?
- Do their actions push the story along?
- Do the minor characters serve a specific purpose?

Theme
- If there is supposed to be a theme, is it apparent?
- Is it subtle?

Style
- Is the writing clear?
- Is the language appropriate for the speaker?

Now get ready to write. In the first prompts you will rely on your imagination as you find yourself walking in strange places or facing tough decisions or encountering unusual people. In the second group of prompts, you will explore your own memories for further ideas. Good luck and good writing!

Part One

Making Things Up

Moe's Café

A detailed description of a place with personality

👉 Start

> You're driving some place far from home when your radiator starts
> steaming. You manage to find a mechanic at a gas station who can fix
> your car, but it's going to take a few hours. You ask him if there's any
> place to get a bite, and he points across the road to Moe's Café. You don't
> have much choice, so you head inside and take a seat at the first booth on
> the left and look around in horror at the filth.

❓ Questions

After reading the prompt above, answer the following questions on another sheet of paper.
Use your answers to help you think about your subject.

1. What does the floor look like?

2. What's on the menu?

3. Who does Blanche, the waitress, resemble?

4. What's hanging on the walls?

5. What's playing on the jukebox? On the TV?

6. What six specific smells can you identify?

7. Moe is cooking behind the counter. What does he look like?

8. You spot Barney, Moe's dog, in the corner. What is he doing?

9. Who are the people sitting in the next booth? What are they talking about?

10. Blanche brings your food. What does it look like?

Getting Ready

In a few sentences, capture the look and the feel of Moe's Café.

 ## Starting Your Story

Now that you have visited Moe's Café, write three ninety-word mini-stories. You'll have to decide who will tell the story, where it will start, and if the tone will be serious or comic. Here are some possibilities.

1. Moe comes up to your table and offers to sell you the place for $200.

2. The waitress whispers to you that she is being held captive.

3. The police charge in and break up an illegal gambling operation in the back.

4. The lady at the table next to you turns out to be your long-lost sister.

5. You find a treasure map on the floor.

6. You play a song on the jukebox and a woman at the counter starts screaming.

7. You suddenly discover a solution to a problem that has been bothering you for months.

OR: Come up with your own idea for a mini-story.

 ## Write Away!

1. Pick the mini-story you like most and make it longer. Consider flashing back to relevant events in your narrator's earlier life.

2. Study your new draft and consider the following: Do the characters seem real? What motivates them? Is there some suspense? Does the setting contribute to the story line?

3. Write the final draft.

 ## Read and Write

Consider reading "A & P" by John Updike, another story in which the setting—in this case a grocery store on the outskirts of a resort community—has a significant effect on the action of the story. Notice how the narrator's "overfamiliarity" with his surroundings contributes to a life-affecting decision. Then create your own story set in a "place with a personality."

 ## On the Screen

Watch *Star Wars: Episode IV* (rated PG) and pay particular attention to the saloon scene on the planet Tatooine. Notice how director George Lucas's attention to detail makes this an unforgettable setting.

> **Today's Special**
>
> Want to see how another student used this prompt to begin a full story? See "Hey, Tom" on page 110.

Mr. Jones's Bad Day

A comic disaster of epic proportions

☞ **Start**

> *Down the street from you lives Mr. Irwin Jones, a quiet, middle-aged man who lives alone and works as a bank teller. Because he works hard and plans well, his life usually goes quite smoothly, if uneventfully. Then one excruciating day, everything goes wrong.*

❓ **Questions**

After reading the prompt above, answer the following questions on another sheet of paper. Use your answers to help you think about your subject. *What happens . . .*

1. right after Mr. Jones's alarm goes off?

2. when he's brushing his teeth?

3. when he's eating his cereal?

4. while he's walking his dog?

5. just before the bus arrives?

6. while he rides the bus?

7. when he greets his first customer?

8. while he eats lunch in the bank cafeteria?

9. at the end of his day?

10. on his way home?

Getting Started

Briefly explain why Mr. Jones had such a terrible day.

 Starting Your Story

Now that you have recorded this poor fellow's misfortunes, write three different ninety-word mini-stories that present the story of Mr. Jones's Bad Day. Notice that simple changes can create significant effects.

1. Write a letter from Mr. Jones to his sister, Trudy, in which he's still really angry.

2. Write a letter from Mr. Jones to his sister, but in this version he thinks the whole thing was pretty funny.

3. Write a letter from Mr. Jones to his sister—this time he thinks he knows why this all happened.

4. This turned out to be a life-changing experience for Mr. Jones. Years later he describes the experience in a chapter from his autobiography.

5. Mr. Jones's house turns out to be haunted. Let the ghost tell the story.

6. Tell this as a children's story starting with the words, "Once upon a time there lived a man named Mr. Jones. . . ."

7. Write a set of directions for someone planning to have a bad day.

OR: Come up with your own idea for a mini-story.

 Write Away!

1. Choose your favorite mini-story and develop it further. Include all the details but add more. Make the scenes more specific. Give Mr. Jones more character.

2. Examine the humor in your new draft. Why is the situation funny? Do unexpected things occur? Do decisions lead to bad outcomes? Do we picture silly images? How should we feel about Mr. Jones? Do we sympathize with him or are we pleased to see him suffer a little?

3. Write the final draft.

 Read and Write

Consider reading "Homecoming" by Garrison Keillor. In this story a father's good intentions lead to increasingly more hilarious results.

 On the Screen

How about having to live your bad day over and over again until you get it right? That's the situation faced by Phil the obnoxious weatherman in the film *Groundhog Day* (rated PG). Notice how the subtle and not-so-subtle variations in Phil's bad day lead at first to comic and then to romantic consequences.

The Final Shot

A moment of heightened suspense

👉 **Start**

> You find yourself inside a gym packed with noisy fans watching a high school basketball play-off game. Three seconds are left and Heyworth Hornet star Jamie Scheets has an open shot from the corner. If he makes it, the home team wins. If he misses, the visiting Pekin Dragons win and eliminate the Hornets from the state tournament. You are sitting in the middle of a section of screaming Hornet fans with a great view of the action.

❓ **Questions**

After reading the prompt above, answer the following questions on another sheet of paper. Use your answers to help you think about your subject.

1. As Jamie gets ready to shoot, what is he doing?

2. What are the Dragon players doing?

3. How are the visiting coach and his players on the bench reacting?

4. What are seven different sounds in the gym that you can identify?

5. What are the Hornet cheerleaders doing?

6. Chester, the local policeman, is standing at the door. How is he behaving?

7. A little old lady is sitting at the end of the aisle. What is she shouting?

8. How do you feel right now?

9. What is the Hornets' coach doing with his hands?

10. What happens when and after he shoots?

Getting Started

Concisely capture this exciting sports scene.

 Starting Your Story

Your head should be filled with the sights, sounds, and smells of the gym. Now write a ninety-word mini-story for three of the following developments. Try to use all of your details.

1. Jamie misses the shot and a riot ensues.

2. You notice a man in front of you stealing the wallet of the man sitting next to him.

3. A stranger suddenly bursts into the gym.

4. You remember something terribly important, and you must leave immediately.

5. Tell the story from the point of view of someone who knows how tough things have been in Heyworth lately.

6. Your cell phone rings, and you must take the call.

7. Someone passes you a note.

OR: Come up with your own idea for a mini-story.

 Write Away!

1. Select your favorite and develop it into a longer story.

2. Study your new draft and consider the following: Is this going to be strictly a sports story, or is it going to be a story that takes place in a sports setting? If it's the former, what have you done to make us care about the outcome? If it's the latter, what is the connection between the game and the story itself?

3. Write the final draft.

 Read and Write

Consider reading "The Pit and the Pendulum" by Edgar Allan Poe. Pay particular attention to Poe's use of sensory detail in establishing tension as he builds to the ultimate climactic moment.

 On the Screen

Enjoy watching *Hoosiers* (rated PG), the fictionalized account of a small rural Indiana town whose local high school team makes it to the state championship. Watch for the detail in the scene in which the team manager/substitute must sink a free throw with the game on the line.

> **Today's Special**
>
> Want to see how another student used this prompt to begin a full story? See "Electricity" on page 112.

Hot Tuesday

Using the setting as a plot catalyst

👉 **Start**

> *It is noon on the hottest day of the year. You are standing at the busiest street corner of the city. Everything and everyone that you see has been influenced by the heat.*

❓ **Questions**

After reading the prompt above, answer the following questions on another sheet of paper. Use your answers to help you think about your subject.

1. How does the heat affect the police officer directing traffic?

2. How are the passengers emerging from a nearby bus reacting to the heat?

3. What smells can you identify?

4. What is the expression on the face of Mrs. Murphy, the woman looking out of her second-floor window?

5. What do your hands look like?

6. Describe the tar on the street. What does it smell like? Look like? Feel like?

7. What sensations are coming from Otto's fruit stand across the street?

8. What do the two nuns walking past you remind you of?

9. Look at Mr. Carson's black Labrador, Buddy, on the corner. What is the heat doing to him?

10. Two cab drivers are arguing—what are they saying?

Getting Started

Recreate this hot spot in a few sentences.

 ## Starting Your Story

Now that you have described this hot place, write three ninety-word mini-stories from the following prompts. In each, the settings you've described above should play an important part. You are . . .

1. looking for an ex-girlfriend/ boyfriend, and you spot her or him.

2. on the run from someone you fear.

3. a detective looking for a bank robber.

4. a novelist trying to overcome writer's block.

5. an alien whose flying saucer is parked in the sewer.

6. a child on an errand for your mother.

7. the policeman's wife worried that her husband is risking a heart attack.

OR: Come up with your own idea for a mini-story.

 ## Write Away!

1. Pick the mini-story you like most and make it longer. Make sure that something happens. Make the setting such a big part of the story that changing the location would alter the plot.

2. Study your new draft. Have you included enough sensory detail to show the effects of the heat?

3. Write the final draft.

 ## Read and Write

Consider reading "To Build a Fire" by Jack London. In this story a man must not only battle the elements in a classic "Man vs. Nature" conflict but also faces an internal conflict as he battles his own inadequacies and growing sense of panic. Note London's vivid use of sensory detail as he recreates the process of freezing to death.

 ## On the Screen

Watch *The Perfect Storm* (rated PG-13). Observe how the storm itself serves as the antagonist in the film, and how sometimes people are at their best under pressure.

High Drama in the Barn

A moment frozen in time

👉 **Start**

> *You are spending the weekend on a farm. On the way back from an early morning walk, you peek into the barn. Inside, a large cat has just cornered a tiny mouse. At that very second the scene is totally still; at any moment violence could erupt. You have an unobstructed view of the scene.*

❓ **Questions**

After reading the prompt above, answer the following questions on another sheet of paper. Use your answers to help you think about your subject.

1. What does the mouse's nose look like?

2. What do the cat's claws resemble?.

3. How is the cat posed?

4. How does the mouse's posture compare to the cat's?

5. What must the cat be thinking?

6. What must the mouse be thinking?

7. What are seven other noises that you can distinguish in the barn?

8. How is the barn lit?

9. What does the entire scene resemble?

10. What previous experience does this prompt you to remember?

Getting Started

Combine your details into a short description of this suspenseful scene.

 Starting Your Story

Now that you've reconstructed the scene, consider these seven possibilities. Then select three and write a ninety-word mini-story for each, including as many details as possible from your answers to the above questions. The twist in this case, however, is that this event has prompted you to take a new direction in your life. As a result of witnessing this scene, you will now . . .

1. marry the person you have been dating for three years.

2. renounce your family fortune.

3. admit your crimes to the police.

4. rehire the man who cheated you.

5. become a monk or hermit.

6. become a veterinarian.

7. invest all of your money in oil.

OR: Come up with your own idea for a mini-story.

 Write Away!

1. Pick your favorite and write a complete short story.

2. Now take your draft and change the narrator. You are now . . .

   • a child who has never imagined anything like this.

   • a sophisticated city dweller.

   • a hardened criminal.

   • an old-timer.

   • the owner of the cat.

3. Write the final draft. The point of view will really matter here.

 Read and Write

Consider reading "Rikki Tikki Tavi" by Rudyard Kipling. Observe how a master storyteller persuades his readers to willingly suspend their disbelief as he draws them into the epic struggle between a pet mongoose and the dangerous pair of cobras that threaten his household.

 On the Screen

Watch the comedy *The Princess Bride* (rated PG). Observe the comic use of tension as the "Dread Pirate Roberts" subdues the swordsman, the giant, and the genius all in succession. You'll enjoy the rich wordplay in this funny movie.

A Distant Land

Creating your own fantasy world

👉 **Start**

> *Stories for children frequently take place in fantastic faraway places like Neverland, Narnia, Hogwarts, or Oz. In this exercise you will create such a place and then tell a story that happens there.*

❓ **Questions**

After reading the prompt above, answer the following questions on another sheet of paper. Use your answers to help you think about your subject.

1. What is the name of your kingdom?

2. How do you get there?

3. What do you notice when you first enter?

4. Who is in charge?

5. How are the laws enforced?

6. How do ordinary people make a living?

7. How do ordinary people spend their free time?

8. Who are the great heroes of the kingdom? The great enemies?

9. What do people hope will happen in the future?

10. What do the people argue about?

Getting Started

Write a two-sentence account of what happens in your distant land.

 Starting Your Story

Take another look at your account of these imaginary events, and then write three ninety-word mini-stories that take place in your kingdom. The action should begin right after one of these events:

1. An enemy force attacks.

2. The leader dies.

3. A stranger arrives.

4. A new invention becomes the rage.

5. A giant storm hits the kingdom.

6. Something popular is banned by the leader.

7. Someone learns to fly.

OR: Come up with your own idea for a mini-story.

 Write Away!

1. Pick the mini-story you like most and fatten it up. Remember that your readers need to care about what happens to your characters.

2. Study your new draft and consider the following: Does your draft contain the traditional elements of a short story? Does the central conflict build to a climax? Is there a possibility for a sequel?

3. Write the final draft.

 Read and Write

Consider reading "Athene's City" by Olivia Coolidge. Notice how in an effective myth elements of both the natural and supernatural blend to create a new story.

 On the Screen

Try watching the film *Finding Neverland* (PG-13), a movie about J. M. Barrie, author of *Peter Pan*. Observe the evolution of Barrie's concept of "Neverland" as it grows from a children's game of "make-believe" to an immensely popular stage play. Notice how the screen writer has blurred the lines between the make-believe world of the "real" and fictional Peters.

Eccentric on the Bus

A detailed account of a chance encounter

👉 Start

> *A stranger sits down next to you on the bus one morning. This person, who at first seems quite normal, turns out to be one of the strangest individuals you have ever met.*

❓ Questions

After reading the prompt above, answer the following questions on another sheet of paper. Use your answers to help you think about your subject.

1. Where are you sitting?

2. At first, what does the stranger appear to be like?

3. What does the stranger say to you?

4. What does the stranger start to read?

5. The stranger suddenly stands up and delivers a speech to the entire bus. What is the speech about? How do people react?

6. The stranger passes you a note. What does it say?

7. The stranger gestures to someone or something outside the window. Describe what the stranger does.

8. The stranger's cell phone rings. What happens next?

9. How does the stranger exit the bus?

10. The stranger hands you a note. You read it and suddenly you understand what's really been going on. What does the note say?

Getting Started

In one long sentence, explain what happened that morning on the bus.

 Starting Your Story

Keeping in mind what you've just written, write three ninety-word mini-stories, each from a different point of view. Try to capture the distinct voice of each narrator. You are . . .

1. a high school student riding to school.

2. a U.S. Marine just back from the war in Iraq.

3. an undercover detective on a case.

4. a senior citizen on her way to the bingo parlor.

5. an escaped convict on the run.

6. an out-of-work English teacher working on a novel.

7. a social worker.

OR: Come up with your own idea for a mini-story.

 Write Away!

1. Choose your favorite and develop it into a complete story. Describe the bus in more detail. Include more of your feelings. Add more dialogue. The ending could be clear or it could be ambiguous.

2. Study your new draft and consider the following: Could your plot be strengthened by expanding the role of one or more of the other passengers on the bus?

3. Write the final draft.

 Read and Write

Consider reading "On the Late Bus" by Susan Engberg. Observe how the presence of the lonely stranger leads the teenage narrator to come to better terms with her own troubles.

 On the Screen

Try watching *What's Eating Gilbert Grape?* (rated PG-13). In Gilbert Grape's family, everyone is eccentric. Observe how the Grapes deal with the townspeople and vice versa.

Someone's Cheating

A moment of truth

👉 **Start**

> *You are a shy, introverted, moral person. You attend a large high school. One day during a math test, you witness the most popular student in the school copying the answers from the student sitting next to you.*

❓ **Questions**

After reading the prompt above, answer the following questions on another sheet of paper. Use your answers to help you think about your subject.

1. What is the school like? What kinds of kids go there? Who are the popular people? Who are left out?

2. How do you fit in? What are your goals?

3. Whom do you respect?

4. Whom don't you respect?

5. Why do you especially hate cheating?

6. What has this particular class been like?

7. Who is the student who cheats?

8. How do you know this student is cheating?

9. Why do you consider doing nothing about it?

10. That night you decide to "do the right thing." What is it?

Getting Started

Briefly report the events leading up to this dilemma.

 ## Starting Your Story

Look one more time at your brief account of the event, and then write a ninety-word mini-story for three of the following situations. It is several years later, and you are explaining to a stranger how your life was altered by this event. You . . .

1. had to leave school.

2. became a hero.

3. decided to have radical plastic surgery.

4. made new friends.

5. joined a new church or religious cult.

6. audition for a reality television program.

7. became a cheater yourself.

OR: Come up with your own idea for a mini-story.

 ## Write Away!

1. Pick the mini-story you like most and turn it into a complete short story. You will need to decide if you want to retain the "story within a story" aspect or to eliminate the stranger as a character.

2. Study your new draft and consider the following: How have you chosen to look back on the past incident? As a flashback? Through dialogue? Is this the most effective method to use?

3. Write the final draft.

 ## Read and Write

Consider reading "Guess What? I Almost Kissed My Father Last Night" by Robert Cormier, author of *The Chocolate War*. Notice how the narrator's misperception of his father's actions ironically leads to a clearer perception later.

 ## On the Screen

Watch *Stand and Deliver* (rated PG), a film about a math teacher in a tough Los Angeles high school whose students' success on the AP Calculus test is so impressive that they are accused of cheating. Pay particular attention to the scene in which the teacher tells the class that they are being forced to retake the test.

Leon the Loner

A look at a man on his own

👉 Start

> *Given a choice, Leon will always choose to be alone. He is a nice enough fellow, but he just prefers his own company.*

❓ Questions

After reading the prompt above, answer the following questions on another sheet of paper. Use your answers to help you think about your subject.

1. Where does Leon work? What are his duties?

2. What is his least favorite childhood memory?

3. How do others regard him?

4. What makes him smile?

5. What law would he like changed?

6. What possession would he least like to lose?

7. Who is his all-time hero?

8. What is his favorite time of day?

9. What was his favorite subject in high school?

10. What section of the newspaper does he read first?

Getting Started

In no more than twenty words, write a character sketch of this solitary figure.

 Starting Your Story

Using as much of this character sketch as you'd like, write a ninety-word mini-story for three of the following:

1. Leon tells about a time he tried but failed to make a friend.

2. Leon describes a time he learned to like and trust one other person.

3. Leon's mother explains why Leon became such a loner.

4. Leon's boss tells what happened when he gave Leon more responsibility.

5. Leon explains why he had no choice but to leave town.

6. Leon describes what happened after he won the lottery.

7. A colleague describes a surprising conversation with Leon.

OR: Come up with your own idea for a mini-story.

 Write Away!

1. Pick the mini-story you like most and develop it into a more complete story. Something must change in Leon's life/perspective.

2. Study your new draft and consider the following: Does Leon's change of heart/circumstances make sense or does it seemed contrived? Is the change a subtle or blatant one?

3. Write the final draft.

 Read and Write

Consider reading "Miss Brill" by Katherine Mansfield. Note how Mansfield sets up a contrast between Miss Brill's perception of the people around her and their true natures.

 On the Screen

Watch the science fiction cult classic *Silent Running* (rated G) about an astronaut who maintains an interplanetary greenhouse. Because the Earth can no longer support plant life, the astronaut is especially devoted to his task. Enjoy the scene in which he unsuccessfully attempts to teach his helper robots to play poker.

Priscilla the Pessimist

A lifetime of glasses half-empty

👉 **Start**

> *Priscilla is a pessimist. If she were a cartoon character, a dark rain cloud would hover over her head at all times. Even when things seem to be going well, she can't enjoy them because she knows that trouble is just around the corner.*

❓ **Questions**

After reading the prompt above, answer the following questions on another sheet of paper. Use your answers to help you think about your subject.

1. How does Priscilla walk? What expression does she wear?

2. What is her normal tone of voice?

3. How does she react to compliments?

4. What kind of clothes does she prefer?

5. What is her job?

6. What is her idea of a pleasant evening?

7. To what clubs and organizations does she belong?

8. What kinds of people does she especially dislike?

9. Who is her favorite historical person?

10. How does she plan to spend her retirement?

Getting Started

Characterize Priscilla in a few sentences.

 Starting Your Story

Now that you have characterized Priscilla in a few words, try writing three ninety-word mini-stories that result from the following events. In each, Priscilla's personality will be tested.

1. Her neighbor decides to turn her into a happy person.

2. She falls in love.

3. She wins the lottery.

4. She is approached by a mime in a restaurant.

5. She gets a promotion.

6. She takes up sculpting.

7. She buys a pet.

OR: Come up with your own idea for a mini-story.

 Write Away!

1. Choose the option you like best and develop it into a longer story. Take care in choosing the narrator. Remember to show why she is such a pessimist. Make sure that something happens.

2. Examine your draft. Is Priscilla a one-dimensional character or does she have notable attributes besides pessimism?

3. Write the final draft.

 Read and Write

Consider reading "I'm a Fool" by Sherwood Anderson. In this turn-of-the-century story, a poor boy lacks the confidence to tell the woman of his dreams his real station in life and instead presents himself to her under false pretenses. Notice the use of ambiguity in the ending—could he have won her heart if she knew his real background?

 On the Screen

Take a look at *Return to Me* (rated PG-13), a romance about a young woman with a heart condition who receives a heart transplant from the deceased wife of an architect.

Juan's New Job

A brand-new take on the world

👉 **Start**

> *Juan comes from a sheltered background. Although he is not rich, he has never really had to provide for himself. When he decides to take a summer job to pay for a car, Juan learns something important and unexpected about himself.*

❓ **Questions**

After reading the prompt above, answer the following questions on another sheet of paper. Use your answers to help you think about your subject.

1. Where does Juan live? What is his daily life like?

2. Before starting his job, how does he see his future?

3. What are his duties at this new job?

4. Who are some of the people who work with Juan? What are they like?

5. How does the job differ from anything he has ever done?

6. What events at work begin to change Juan?

7. What is the nature of the change? New knowledge? New attitude? New skills?

8. How does he now view the future?

9. How does this change affect his personal life?

10. What does he say to his boss on the last day of work?

Getting Started

How was Juan changed by his new job? Answer in two sentences.

 Starting Your Story

You know the essentials. Now write a ninety-word mini-story for three of the following. Keep in mind that the point of view will be an important factor in assessing the effects of the change. Tell the story . . .

1. from Juan's point of view.

2. from Juan's father's point of view.

3. from the point of view of Charlie, an old-timer who has worked for the company for years.

4. from the point of view of Anita, Juan's steady girlfriend, who is not pleased with the "new Juan."

5. as a series of entries from Juan's diary.

6. in a series of letters between Juan's boss and the high school counselor, who had urged Juan to take this job.

7. in a single scene.

OR: Come up with your own idea for a mini-story.

 Write Away!

1. Choose your favorite and expand it into a longer story: develop your characters, heighten the scenes, and build more suspense.

2. Study your new draft and consider the following: Has the change been too easy? Would making the change more subtle add to the realism of the story?

3. Write the final draft.

 Read and Write

Consider reading "The Tail" by Joyce Hansen, a story about Tasha, a young girl who must baby-sit her younger brother for a whole summer. Notice how the experience not only makes Tasha a better baby-sitter, but also a better sister.

 On the Screen

Watch the film *Running on Empty* (rated PG-13), a film about former anti-war activists wanted by the FBI who have been living underground—and raising a family—since the 1960s. As a result, they must continually adopt entirely new identities and start fresh in new locations. Observe the early scene in which their cover is blown and they must leave yet another new home behind.

Too Much Person

A case of excess

☞ **Start**

> *Imagine someone with too much of a good quality. This could be compassion, intelligence, pride, honesty, or any other trait we normally praise.*

❓ **Questions**

After reading the prompt above, answer the following questions on another sheet of paper. Use your answers to help you think about your subject.

1. How does this quality reveal itself?

2. Who is TMP's (Too Much Person's) hero or role model?

3. What is TMP's worst nightmare?

4. Who is TMP's favorite TV character?

5. What is TMP's favorite childhood memory?

6. Where does TMP like to spend his or her vacation?

7. What makes TMP really mad?

8. Who are some of TMP's enemies?

9. What big mistake does TMP make? What huge problem does this create?

10. What are the difficult choices TMP must make? What are his or her options? What does TMP decide to do? What happens?

Getting Started

Write a brief but detailed personality profile of this extreme figure.

 Starting Your Story

Keeping in mind what you have just written about this unique character, write three of the following as ninety-word mini-stories. Tell the story . . .

1. from the point of view of an all-knowing neighbor.

2. from the point of view of someone who has recently moved next door to TMP.

3. from the third-person omniscient point of view, starting at the point when the bad decision is made and then flashing back to explain the circumstances.

4. in a letter from TMP to a friend explaining how this has been a learning experience.

5. in a letter in which it is clear that TMP has not learned a lesson from this experience.

6. as a children's tale beginning "Once upon a time. . . ."

7. as a comic play.

OR: Come up with your own idea for a mini-story.

 Write Away!

1. Choose the strongest mini-story and develop it. Spend more time on the beginning. Add more character description to the exposition. Describe the scenes more vividly.

2. Study your new draft and consider the following: Does the nature of TMP's quality match the tone of your story? Should your readers be amused? Shocked? Dismayed? Moved?

3. Write the final draft.

 Read and Write

Consider reading "Betty" by Margaret Atwood, the story of a seemingly "Not Enough Person." Notice the author's emphasis on learning—the narrator is still attempting to gain insight into Betty's situation years after Betty's death.

 On the Screen

Enjoy *Liar, Liar* (rated PG-13), a comedy about a lawyer whose son's birthday wish is for his father to stop telling lies. Notice the response of those around him to his newfound honesty.

Wacky Situation

A dog's dilemma

👉 **Start**

> *You are an old dog named Doris. You and your husband Fred and Little Doris live happily with the Millers. Now suddenly you face a difficult problem, one that could mean the end of your family.*

❓ Questions

After reading the prompt above, answer the following questions on another sheet of paper. Use your answers to help you think about your subject.

1. Where do you and your family sleep at night?

2. How do you spend your day?

3. Why are the Millers especially good owners?

4. What is life like for pets with mean owners?

5. What big problem do you now face?

6. If you don't solve it, what might happen to your family?

7. What might happen to the Millers?

8. Why do you think you can solve it?

9. What do you decide to do?

10. What happens?

Getting Started

Recreate this odd episode in a few sentences.

 Starting Your Story

How can you now turn all this weirdness into a story? Try writing three ninety-word mini-stories, each with the different plot ingredient provided. Doris and Fred must . . .

1. go to the big city.

2. use a time machine.

3. listen in on a phone conversation.

4. read the Millers' mail.

5. learn to speak French.

6. don a disguise.

7. enlist the help of other pets.

OR: Come up with your own idea for a mini-story.

 Write Away!

1. Choose your favorite mini-story and write a full story with Doris as a narrator.

2. Study your new draft and consider the following: What have you done to get your readers to care about Doris's predicament? How have you attempted to get your readers to "suspend their disbelief" over the fact that your narrator is a problem-solving canine?

3. Write the final draft.

 Read and Write

Consider reading "The Secret Life of Walter Mitty" by James Thurber. In this little gem of a story, Thurber creates literature's most famous daydreamer. Notice the humor of Mitty's daydreams and the funny/not-so-funny realities that drive him to live in a dream world.

 On the Screen

Enjoy the film *Babe* (rated G), the story of a pig who longs to work as a sheepdog. Notice how the film compels us to suspend our disbelief and become involved in the lives of both the human and non-human inhabitants of the farm.

Brenda's Solution

Getting by with a little help from a friend

👉 **Start**

> *Brenda and Lucy are best friends. Each has sworn to "always be there" for the other one. When Lucy comes to Brenda with a particular problem, Brenda has a chance to show what a true friend she really is.*

❓ **Questions**

After reading the prompt above, answer the following questions on another sheet of paper. Use your answers to help you think about your subject.

1. Who are the girls? Where do they live? How do they know each other?

2. What is Lucy's problem? What will happen if she doesn't solve it?

3. Who is to blame for the problem?

4. Before talking to Brenda, how did Lucy try to handle the problem herself?

5. What was Brenda's first reaction upon hearing of Lucy's dilemma?

6. What was her first suggestion?

7. What does Brenda finally decide to do?

8. Why does it first appear that her plan will fail?

9. Why does it finally succeed?

10. How has Lucy's life improved? How do they know each other?

Getting Started

Explain briefly how Brenda saved the day.

 Starting Your Story

Now that you have summarized Brenda's good deed, try writing it as a ninety-word mini-story. Choose three ideas below. In each case you will tell the story from a different point of view. Tell the story from the point of view of . . .

1. another friend, who has been convinced that there is no solution.

2. another friend whose life had earlier benefited from Brenda's advice.

3. Lucy in the present tense.

4. Brenda looking back twenty years later.

5. a driver's education teacher who had both girls as students.

6. a journalist who interviews both girls.

7. Brenda's mother in prison.

OR: Come up with your own idea for a mini-story.

 Write Away!

1. Choose your favorite mini-story and develop it further. Make sure that something is at stake for the characters.

2. Study your new draft and consider the following: Does each of the girls have a distinct personality? Try using dialogue to establish their uniqueness.

3. Write the final draft.

 Read and Write

Consider reading "Initiation," a story about teenage cliques written by Sylvia Plath while she was still a teenager herself. Although this story was first published in 1950, the choice Millicent must make between popularity and integrity remains timeless.

 On the Screen

Watch the film *Fried Green Tomatoes* (rated PG-13). In this story within a story, notice how the good people of Whistle Stop, Alabama, concoct a particularly unique remedy to the troublesome problem of Ruth's abusive husband.

Coach's Dilemma

A story of decisions and consequences

👉 **Start**

> *You are a successful high school coach. Yesterday, however, you found yourself in a tough situation and acted very badly. As a result, you lost the respect of your players. Now what?*

? Questions

After reading the prompt above, answer the following questions on another sheet of paper. Use your answers to help you think about your subject.

1. What do you coach?

2. In what ways have you been a successful coach?

3. What is your reputation?

4. What tough situation did you face yesterday?

5. What were your choices?

6. Why was your decision wrong?

7. What were the bad consequences?

8. What are your choices now?

9. What do you decide to do?

10. How well does this work?

Getting Started

Retell this agonizing story in a few sentences.

 Starting Your Story

Keeping in mind what you have just written, write a ninety-word mini-story for three of these seven possible outcomes. Your plan . . .

1. backfires and you quit coaching forever.

2. seems to work, but you still are not satisfied.

3. is a moderate success, but you still have work to do.

4. is a great success.

5. teaches you something you did not expect to learn about young people.

6. teaches you something important about yourself.

7. creates even bigger problems for you.

OR: Come up with your own idea for a mini-story.

 Write Away!

1. Pick the mini-story you like best and develop it into a complete short story.

2. Study your new draft and consider the following: Are the coach's situation and subsequent actions believable? Do the characters respond the way people you know might respond?

3. Write the final draft.

 Read and Write

Consider reading "Tularecito" by John Steinbeck. In this story a well-meaning teacher does more harm than good when she attempts to reach out to a special student. Note the contrast between her perspective and that of Tularecito's guardian.

 On the Screen

Take a look at *Remember the Titans* (rated PG), the story of an African-American football coach who takes over a newly integrated football program. Watch how the concept of "team" evolves over the course of the season.

Burned-out Teacher

Taking a second chance at life

👉 **Start**

> *You are a student whose favorite teacher is about to retire. She has been an excellent teacher in the past, but now it appears that it is time for her to go. Today, however, the teacher surprises everyone by showing people she can still teach.*

❓ **Questions**

After reading the prompt above, answer the following questions on another sheet of paper. Use your answers to help you think about your subject.

1. Who is the teacher? Name? School subject?

2. What kind of school does she teach in? (size, student body, etc.)

3. Why did she go into teaching?

4. Why was she such a great success up until she turned 60?

5. What happened at 60 years old to make her think she was losing her touch?

6. How did the students, other teachers, administrators, and her husband react to her aging?

7. What surprising development keeps her from quitting?

8. What does she do to show she is not quite done yet?

9. How do others react to her new energy?

10. What does she do now that she has regained some energy and purpose?

Getting Started

Give an overview of this pivotal moment in the teacher's career.

 ## Starting Your Story

There has to be a story here. Start by writing three ninety-word mini-stories for three of the following suggestions.

1. Tell the story from the teacher's point of view.

2. Tell the story from the point of view of her most loyal student.

3. Start in the middle of the story.

4. Change the tone of the story from serious to comic (or vice versa).

5. Shift the climax to a different moment.

6. Compose the story entirely in dialogue between two teachers in the faculty lounge.

7. Write the story in a letter from her husband to his best friend in Omaha.

OR: Come up with your own idea for a mini-story.

 ## Write Away!

1. Pick the mini-story you like best and make it longer. Develop the characters more fully. Describe the setting more vividly. Try adding a subplot.

2. Study your new draft and consider the following: What motivates your characters? Have you *shown* rather than *told about* the situation? Are there elements of suspense?

3. Write the final draft.

 ## Read and Write

Consider reading "Black and Tan" by Madison Smartt Bell. In this story a crusty loner has the opportunity to impact the lives of troubled juvenile delinquents. Notice Bell's use of ambiguity as the protagonist questions the value of what he has done.

 ## On the Screen

Watch *The Man without a Face* (rated PG-13), the story of a former teacher who struggles to deal with life after he has been disfigured in a car accident. Observe how his reluctant agreement to tutor a troubled boy leads to both positive and negative consequences.

> **Today's Special**
>
> Want to see how another student used this prompt to begin a full story? See "Evanescence" on page 114.

Betrayal

Integrating theme with plot

👉 **Start**

> *You run a small business. You are liked and respected by both customers and employees. Then one day you discover that Donald, someone you have always trusted, has betrayed you.*

❓ **Questions**

After reading the prompt above, answer the following questions on another sheet of paper. Use your answers to help you think about your subject.

1. Who are you? What does your company do?

2. What is Donald's job?

3. Why have you always been pleased with his work?

4. What is he doing behind your back?

5. How did you find out?

6. What was your immediate reaction? How did you feel? What did you say?

7. Who did you consult?

8. What was your first choice of action?

9. What was another choice?

10. What should you do and why?

Getting Started

Summarize the moments leading up to and immediately after the betrayal.

 ## Starting Your Story

Keep all those moments in mind and then write a ninety-word mini-story for three of these outcomes. Experiment with different points of view: yours, your wife's, another worker's, and Donald's.

1. Donald admits his crime, apologizes, and returns to work a better person.

2. Donald denies his crime and leaves.

3. You discover that Donald had a reason for betraying you and you forgive him.

4. You discover that it was really your own fault; he had no choice but to betray you.

5. Your choice of action fails. You sell the business and move away.

6. Your choice of action fails, but along the way you learn how to make the company even more successful.

7. Your choice of action succeeds. Donald leaves the company and eventually does something even worse.

OR: Come up with your own idea for a mini-story.

 ## Write Away!

1. Pick the mini-story you like most and develop it around one of these themes:

   • Life is fair.

   • Life is not fair.

   • Appearances lie.

   • People never change.

   • We don't understand our own motives.

   • We don't like to admit our mistakes.

2. Study your new draft and consider the following: How have you presented your theme? Is it stated outright or do your readers have to figure it out for themselves?

3. Write the final draft.

 ## Read and Write

Consider reading "The Lie" by Kurt Vonnegut. In this story Eli really lets the family down: He not only fails to meet the admission standards at prestigious Whitehill Academy, but he also tears up the rejection letter before his parents can read it. Note Vonnegut's use of irony at the end—just who has betrayed whom in this story?

 ## On the Screen

Try *Silverado* (rated PG-13), a Western about a man who must decide whether he wants to play it safe or to stand by his friends in their time of danger. Pay attention to the scene in the saloon when Stella, the tiny proprietor, gets angry at the "bullies" in the world.

Playing Parent

Taking a walk on the wild side

👉 Start

> You are a suburban parent with an agreeable daughter who is doing well in school. You are pleased with her success, but you fear she is growing up naïve. You decide to do something that will make her more aware, but you don't want to be too obvious.

❓ Questions

After reading the prompt above, answer the following questions on another sheet of paper. Use your answers to help you think about your subject.

1. Who are you? Where do you live?

2. How did your childhood compare with your daughter's? Why do you know something about the tougher side of life?

3. In what ways has your daughter been a strong student?

4. How does your daughter spend her time outside of school?

5. What are your daughter's friends like?

6. What has your daughter said lately that concerns you?

7. What has she done lately that also concerns you?

8. What has been happening in the city?

9. What courses of action do you consider?

10. What do you finally decide to do? Why?

Getting Started

Briefly restate the key pieces in this little story.

 Starting Your Story

Take what you started and develop it into three different ninety-word mini-stories, each from the parent's point of view and each beginning with one of these following seven sentences:

1. I probably should have known better.

2. I thought I knew my daughter, but I was so wrong.

3. Looking back, I guess we both learned something.

4. I had tried to make my intentions clear.

5. Now it's her turn to teach me something.

6. Now I see why she was so pleasant.

7. Sometimes things are exactly as they appear.

OR: Come up with your own idea for a mini-story.

 Write Away!

1. Pick the approach you like best and develop it further. You will need to consider whether or not the daughter will ever realize her parent's involvement in her learning experience.

2. Study your new draft and consider the following: Does the tone of the story—comic, serious, ironic, and so on—work well with the lesson learned by the daughter and/or the parent?

3. Write the final draft.

 Read and Write

Consider reading "I Stand Here Ironing" by Tillie Olsen, a realistic, first-person story of a mother who regrets that she may not be able to give one of her daughters the attention she needs. Observe how the narrator attempts to *iron out* this family crisis while ironing the family's clothes.

 On the Screen

Try renting the film *Bless the Beasts and the Children* (1971 version; rated PG). Based on the novel by Glendon Swarthout, this film tells the story of six troubled suburban kids who are sent by their parents to a camp whose motto is "Send us a boy and we'll send you back a cowboy!" Notice how the boys do mature, but not necessarily in the way their parents intended.

Teacher Done You Wrong

A conflict of wills

👉 **Start**

> *Your U.S. history teacher, Mr. Mellonig, does not seem to like you. His comments are sarcastic. He rarely calls on you; and when he does, he smirks at your answer. After you receive a C– in his class, you decide to do something drastic.*

❓ Questions

After reading the prompt above, answer the following questions on another sheet of paper. Use your answers to help you think about your subject.

1. Who are you? What kind of school do you attend?

2. What's Mr. Mellonig's reputation?

3. Why do you think you should receive a higher grade?

4. How have you been successful in previous classes?

5. When did you first suspect Mr. Mellonig was picking on you?

6. What was another example of unfair treatment?

7. What advice do you get from your counselor? From your friends?

8. What happens on the final test?

9. What three courses of action do you consider taking?

10. What do you finally do?

Getting Started

Briefly answer these questions: Who? What? Where? When? and Why?

 Starting Your Story

Take what you've just written and turn it into a longer story. Begin by writing a ninety-word mini-story for three of the following. In each you are telling this event to someone many years later to illustrate that this observation is something you deeply believe.

1. People can be stubborn.

2. Sometimes it pays to be pushy.

3. It's good to be careful.

4. People can change.

5. There's more to life than meets the eye.

6. School is different from real life.

7. Teachers are people, too.

OR: Come up with your own idea for a mini-story.

 Write Away!

1. Choose your favorite and expand it into a fully developed short story. The thematic element of this one will be especially important.

2. Study your new draft and consider the following: Is the thematic message subtle or heavy-handed? Are you preaching to your readers or letting them draw their own conclusions?

3. Write the final draft.

 Read and Write

Consider reading "Eleven" by Sandra Cisneros, the story of a young girl's birthday gone wrong. Observe how as the narrator's day falls apart, the crabby teacher manages to make a bad situation worse.

 On the Screen

Watch *Dead Poet's Society* (rated PG), the story of Mr. Keating, an unconventional English teacher in an extremely conventional New England prep school. Notice how the director uses a montage of the students' various classes to establish the contrast between Keating's approach and that of his colleagues.

Luck at the Beach

A detailed account of a life-altering moment

👉 Start

> *You believe that luck is all that matters. Good efforts are not rewarded, and bad ones are rarely punished. Therefore, you lack the motivation to try very hard. Then one day at the beach you change your mind.*

❓ Questions

After reading the prompt above, answer the following questions on another sheet of paper. Use your answers to help you think about your subject.

1. Who are you and what do you do for a living? Why are you spending the day at the beach?

2. What recent event from last week confirms your conviction that life is all about luck?

3. At the beach you spot an old friend. How does this encounter alter your view about luck?

4. What have you just read in the newspaper that surprises you?

5. A stranger asks you for a favor. What is it?

6. A lady next to you is talking on a cell phone. What is she saying?

7. Children nearby are building a sand castle. After watching them carefully, what do you observe?

8. What happens when you go for a swim?

9. You suddenly remember something that happened to you back in kindergarten. What was it and what prompted the memory?

10. On the way out of the parking lot, you decide to do something you have never done before. What is that something and what does it have to do with luck?

Getting Started

Compose a quick account of the events of this singular day.

 Starting Your Story

Try turning the quick account into a story. Begin by writing three ninety-word mini-stories about what happened at the beach. For each story, one of the elements listed below is most crucial in creating your new view of luck.

1. the sand castle

2. the lady on the cell phone

3. your old friend

4. swimming

5. the stranger's request

6. the article in the paper

7. the kindergarten flashback

OR: Come up with your own idea for a mini-story.

 Write Away!

1. Pick the mini-story you like most and make it longer. Consider flashing back to relevant events in your earlier life.

2. Study your new draft. Does it give us a sense of what it feels like to be you? Is the change subtle or obvious?

3. Write the final draft.

 Read and Write

Consider reading "The Monkey's Paw" by W. W. Jacobs. In this frequently anthologized tale of horror, a married couple gets more than it bargained for when they are granted three wishes from a magical source. Note the use of contrast between what they wished for and what the paw actually granted them.

 On the Screen

Try watching *You've Got Mail* (rated PG-13), starring Tom Hanks and Meg Ryan. In this romantic comedy, a little bit of luck and the magic of the Internet help to transform two bitter business rivals first into pen pals and then into soul mates. Notice how Tom Hanks's discovery of his pen pal's identity provides him with the head start he needs to get his own life together before he becomes part of Meg Ryan's.

> **Today's Special**
>
> Want to see how another student used this prompt to begin a full story? See "A Stranger's Request" on page 107.

Risking It All for a Friend

A detailed account of putting it on the line

👉 **Start**

> *A life-long friend needs your help. Even though helping this person will be risky, you know that you must try. Not everyone, however, sees it your way.*

❓ **Questions**

After reading the prompt above, answer the following questions on another sheet of paper. Use your answers to help you think about your subject.

1. Who are you?

2. In what ways are you a normal sort of person?

3. Who is your friend?

4. Why has your friendship been so strong?

5. Why is your friend in trouble?

6. What will happen if your friend is not helped?

7. What do you try to do?

8. Why does the plan at first seem to be working?

9. What snags do you encounter?

10. What finally happens?

Getting Started

Draft a concentrated version of this adventure.

 Starting Your Story

Now, take this brief version and write a ninety-word mini-story from three of the following perspectives. Tell the story from . . .

1. your point of view in the present tense.

2. your point of view a day later.

3. your point of view years later.

4. your friend's point of view in the present tense.

5. your friend's point of view a day later.

6. a different friend's point of view many years later.

7. the point of view of an outsider reporting what others have told him.

OR: Come up with your own idea for a mini-story.

 Write Away!

1. Choose your favorite and build it into a complete story. Be sure the decision has real consequences.

2. Study your new draft and consider the following: Is the ending too predictable? Try adding an unexpected twist to the way things turn out.

3. Write the final draft.

 Read and Write

Consider reading "Fan Club," a story by Rona Maynard about the power of peer pressure. In this story a high school girl named Laura must choose between doing the popular thing and doing the right thing. Notice the similarity in the situations between this story and the story "Initiation" by Sylvia Plath (see "Brenda's Solution").

 On the Screen

Watch the ultimate "risking it all" movie—*Rocky* (rated PG). Focus on the scene in which Rocky first rejects, then accepts, Mickey's offer to be Rocky's manager.

False Charge

A detailed account of a dangerous situation

👉 Start

> *You have just been accused of something you did not do. You consider your options and finally decide how you must act.*

❓ Questions

After reading the prompt above, answer the following questions on another sheet of paper. Use your answers to help you think about your subject.

1. Who are you? What is your age? Your profession? Your family situation?

2. Why are you so highly regarded in the community?

3. Of what have you been accused?

4. What is the evidence against you?

5. What actually happened?

6. Why is it difficult to prove your innocence?

7. What will happen if your name is not cleared?

8. What are your choices?

9. What do you decide to do?

10. Do you succeed?

Getting Started

Blend all of your answers into a concise version of this incident.

 Starting Your Story

Take this concentrated version and make it longer. Start by writing a ninety-word mini-story for three of the following possibilities. Begin each with the sentence: "I knew it was a dangerous thing to do, but I had to do something."

1. Your plan succeeds and your name is cleared.

2. Your plan succeeds, but doubt remains.

3. Your plan doesn't succeed, but at least you tried.

4. Your plan fails, and you are punished for this crime you didn't commit.

5. At the last minute you come up with a new idea that clears your name.

6. At the last minute you come up with a new idea that makes matters even worse.

7. Before you act, some new event makes your "crime" seem unimportant.

OR: Come up with your own idea for a mini-story.

 Write Away!

1. Pick the alternative you like most and make it longer. Consider flashing back to relevant events in your earlier relationship with the accuser.

2. Study your new draft and consider the following: Are the emotions powerful? Does the plan seem realistic or contrived?

3. Write the final draft.

 Read and Write

Consider reading "Teenage Wasteland" by Joyce Carol Oates. In this story a well-meaning but ineffectual mother struggles to trust a teenage son who does little to earn that trust. Note Oates's avoidance of easy answers and pat endings.

 On the Screen

Watch the film classic *To Kill a Mockingbird* (not rated). Despite community pressure, Southern lawyer Atticus Finch agrees to defend a black man falsely accused of assaulting a white woman. Pay particular attention to the power of the language in Finch's summation speech to the jury.

Gatsby

A tale of love and loss

👉 Start

> *Imagine that you are in the same predicament as the famous literary millionaire Jay Gatsby—you are a man who can never get over the lost love of your life. The loss destroys you.*

❓ Questions

After reading the prompt above, answer the following questions on another sheet of paper. Use your answers to help you think about your subject.

1. Who are you?

2. In what ways have you been hugely successful?

3. How do people explain your great success?

4. Who is the love of your life?

5. How did you first meet?

6. What first attracted her to you?

7. How did your relationship succeed for a little while?

8. Why did you break up?

9. How have your efforts to renew the relationship failed?

10. What is the sad outcome?

Getting Started

Restate the entire happening in two sentences.

 Starting Your Story

Look again at your summary of events and then write three ninety-word mini-stories, each from a different vantage point. Write the story from . . .

1. your point of view as if the event just happened and you're describing it to someone you know well.

2. your point of view as if the event happened years ago. Explain why this lost romance was so significant to your life.

3. your point of view in the present tense as if you are still living through the tragedy.

4. the woman's point of view in a letter to a mutual friend.

5. the woman's point of view many years after the break-up.

6. the point of view of someone who knows both of you well.

7. from the point of view of someone who is hurt by what happened.

OR: Come up with your own idea for a mini-story.

 Write Away!

1. Pick the mini-story you like most and develop it further by adding detail and rounding out the characters. Avoid being melodramatic—strive for conveying sincere emotions.

2. Study your new draft and consider the following: How are your readers meant to feel about your characters? Is someone the villain of the piece or is each of the characters partially to blame? Are they the victims of bad luck or are they just not well-suited for one another?

3. Write the final draft.

 Read and Write

Consider reading "A Mother in Mannville" by Marjorie Kinnan Rawlings, the story of a woman writer who hires an orphan boy to do odd jobs. As he works for her, the boy starts to imagine that their relationship is closer than it really is. Decide how you think the woman should have handled the situation.

 On the Screen

Watch *Pretty in Pink* (rated PG-13), the story of a poor girl who is drawn into the glamorous lifestyle of the rich. Determine if her friends and enemies are realistically portrayed or if you think they are merely teenage movie stereotypes.

Grandma Reconsiders

A bittersweet reflection

👉 **Start**

> *You are an eighty-five-year-old great grandmother who has just been moved into a nursing home. You find yourself thinking about your four sons. The oldest three have made you proud. The youngest, Jason, has been much harder to love; but now as you think more about Jason, you start to realize that maybe—just maybe—he really loved you the most of all.*

❓ **Questions**

After reading the prompt above, answer the following questions on another sheet of paper. Use your answers to help you think about your subject. How can each of the following instances of Jason's apparently unacceptable behavior be seen in a more positive light? Jason's . . .

1. messy clothes?

2. unfriendly companions?

3. unwillingness to banter at dinner?

4. filthy car?

5. loud arguments with his siblings?

6. refusal to attend his own graduation?

7. choice of work over college?

8. disdain for authority figures?

9. unfriendly pets?

10. unwillingness to laugh at jokes?

Getting Started

How does the world now look to Grandma? Answer briefly.

 Starting Your Story

Now that you have looked at the world through Grandma's eyes, write three ninety-word mini-stories that explore Grandma's relationship with her family. Try to imagine how an eighty-five-year-old woman might view such matters. Write . . .

1. a letter to Jason discussing your change of heart.

2. an entry in your diary explaining how you now realize how insincere your other sons have been.

3. a series of e-mails between you and Jason.

4. a series of short letters between you and one of the other sons.

5. a third-person story that begins, "Now she finally understood why Jason had given her a bowling ball for her seventy-fifth birthday."

6. a letter to your lawyer explaining how and why you wish to change your will.

7. a monologue that begins, "I hope it's not too late . . . ."

OR: Come up with your own idea for a mini-story.

 Write Away!

1. Choose your favorite and develop it into a longer story about the grandmother's realization. Consider using dialogue to contrast the various characters' subjective memories of these incidents.

2. Study your new draft and consider the following: Does your setting play a significant role in the story? Are the characters rounded or one-dimensional (the greedy one, the weak one, the dreamer, etc.)? Is the reconciliation too easy?

3. Write the final draft.

 Read and Write

Consider reading "Everyday Use" by Alice Walker, author of *The Color Purple*. In this story a mother comes to realize that for years she has been favoring the wrong daughter. Notice how the mother's handmade quilts serve as a physical symbol of her motherly love.

 On the Screen

Take a look at *Field of Dreams* (rated PG), a baseball fantasy film based on the novel *Shoeless Joe* by W. P. Kinsella. In this film an Iowa farmer gets the chance to reunite and reconnect with his deceased father with the help of a little magic and a little baseball. Pay particular attention to the scenes in which Ray discusses the rift between his father and himself and the game of catch they are able to play at the end of the film.

Part Two

Remembering Things

Old Acquaintance/New Role

Transforming a character

👉 **Start**

> *Create a character based closely on someone you know well. Then place that real character into a totally new situation.*

❓ **Questions**

After reading the prompt above, answer the following questions on another sheet of paper. Use your answers to help you think about your subject.

1. Who is this person?

2. Why do you know this person so well?

3. What might be this person's worst nightmare?

4. What book might this person write?

5. For what job is this person uniquely suited?

6. Who could be this person's enemies?

7. What is this person's favorite TV show?

8. Where would this person never live?

9. What slogan would this person have hanging on the wall?

10. What might be this person's favorite childhood memory?

Getting Started

Write a short, complete sketch of this familiar person.

 Starting Your Story

Think about a strong quality your sketch reveals and then write three ninety-word mini-stories that put your person in a difficult situation. Notice that your character now has a new role in life. Your person is . . .

1. a high school principal who bans card playing in the cafeteria.

2. a single parent who sends his or her son to military school.

3. a poker player who has quit smoking.

4. a popular athlete who marries the class clown.

5. a biology teacher who brings a snake to class.

6. a minister who invites an atheist to deliver the weekly sermon.

7. a social worker whose eighty-year-old uncle moves in.

OR: Come up with your own idea for a mini-story.

 Write Away!

1. Choose your favorite mini-story and develop it. Remember this is a real person you have placed in a new situation.

2. Study your new draft and consider the following: Is the situation too farfetched? Would a mutual friend recognize this person from your profile?

3. Write the final draft.

 Read and Write

Consider reading "The Laughing Man" by J. D. Salinger. In this story the author of *The Catcher in the Rye* creates the unforgettable "Chief"—a storyteller of epic proportions. Note how the tone of this story abruptly changes as the Chief's real life starts to impact his fictional one.

 On the Screen

Watch scenes from the comedies *Tootsie* (rated PG), *Mrs. Doubtfire* (rated PG-13), and *Some Like It Hot* (rated PG). In each, men masquerade as women and in the process learn something about themselves. Be on the lookout for contrasts in comic approach that lead to differences in the overall tone of each film.

Great Teacher

A detailed account of a life-altering moment

👉 **Start**

> *Recall a teacher you greatly admired. This could be a classroom instructor who taught you to read or the coach who taught you how to high jump. No matter what the particulars, this person ranks as one of your all-time favorites.*

❓ **Questions**

After reading the prompt above, answer the following questions on another sheet of paper. Use your answers to help you think about your subject.

1. What and where did this person teach?

2. What was this teacher's reputation?

3. What was your very first experience with this teacher?

4. When did you first realize this person was such a fine teacher?

5. What's a later example of this teacher's excellence?

6. How did this person deal with unwilling students?

7. How did the teacher handle difficult material?

8. For what other jobs was this person suited?

9. For what type of job was this person least suited?

10. Who should play this person in a movie?

Getting Started

Shape all of your details into a profile of this extraordinary educator.

 Starting Your Story

Keeping in mind these positive memories, write three ninety-word mini-stories, each revealing how your teacher would react to a crisis.

1. There is a shooting in the cafeteria.

2. The teacher's son is caught stealing from a local store.

3. Another teacher has physically abused a student.

4. Someone spreads a damaging rumor about this teacher.

5. The teacher's spouse has a serious disease.

6. The new principal wants to get rid of this teacher.

7. The teacher catches a favorite student cheating.

OR: Come up with your own idea for a mini-story.

 Write Away!

1. Pick your favorite and develop it by resolving the problem. Remember that even though you will be relying on your imagination, your main character is based on someone from real life and should act accordingly.

2. Study your new draft and consider the following: Is the resolution to the conflict a realistic one?

3. Write the final draft.

 Read and Write

Consider reading "A Lesson in Discipline" by Teresa Foley. In this story we learn that appearances can be deceiving as an unbending school teacher comes in contact with a tough, young troublemaker. Note the use of the first-person observer point of view—the narrator is a class member, but we never really learn who he or she is.

 On the Screen

Watch the film *Mr. Holland's Opus* (rated PG), the story of a high school music teacher who evolves from a reluctant newcomer into a local legend. Pay particular attention to the pivotal scene in which he convinces the red-haired clarinet player to "play the sunset."

Savvy Acquaintance

A detailed account of someone special

👉 **Start**

> A "savvy" person might not be smart in a traditional school way, but this person can figure out how to avoid problems or, if necessary, to solve them. Who is the savviest person you know? Perhaps this person is someone older, someone who has been around long enough to figure things out.

❓ **Questions**

After reading the prompt above, answer the following questions on another sheet of paper. Use your answers to help you think about your subject.

1. What does this person do?

2. What is your relationship?

3. How do you happen to know so much about this person?

4. Do others agree with your view?

5. What's an example of this person's cleverness?

6. What's another example?

7. What's one more example?

8. What might this person do in an emergency?

9. What would be a perfect job for this person?

10. What job wouldn't work?

Getting Started

Capture this intriguing personality in twenty words.

 Starting Your Story

Think about all of the ways this person is so savvy and then write three ninety-word mini-stories, each of which fictionalizes this person. Begin each story with the options listed below. Your person . . .

1. meets a direct opposite.

2. is asked to solve a crime.

3. falls in love.

4. gets fired.

5. turns sixty-five years old.

6. takes a trip to China.

7. makes a call to a psychic hotline.

OR: Come up with your own idea for a mini-story.

 Write Away!

1. Pick the mini-story you like most and make it longer by adding detail and dialogue. Further develop your person's abilities, but keep them based on real-life character traits.

2. Study your new draft and consider the following: How well do this character's traits translate to this new situation? Is your person still as impressive? Do you still recognize your original person in this new fictional character?

3. Write the final draft.

 Read and Write

Consider reading "The Right Thing" by Stephen Stark. Set in a trailer camp, this story tells of a young man who learns from his father that compassion is not weakness and force is not strength.

 On the Screen

Try watching the film *American Graffiti* (rated PG), directed by *Star Wars* director George Lucas. Observe how the local drag-racing legend, John Milner, deals with yet another generation of friends who are going to go on with their lives and leave him behind.

One of a Kind

A sketch of a very real character

👉 **Start**

> *We all know unique people. Who is the most unforgettable person you know? Is this a friend from school? A colleague from work? Perhaps it's a family member or someone you knew briefly long ago.*

❓ **Questions**

After reading the prompt above, answer the following questions on another sheet of paper. Use your answers to help you think about your subject.

1. How do you know this person?

2. Based on this person's background, what would people expect this person to be like?

3. What is an instance of this person's unique behavior?

4. What is another instance?

5. What is a third instance?

6. How would this person handle a real crisis?

7. How would this person react to winning the lottery?

8. Do all people see this person as you do?

9. What has this person taught you about life?

10. What should appear on this person's gravestone?

Getting Started

Write a biographical sketch of your unique character.

 Starting Your Story

Try fictionalizing this unique character. Begin by writing three ninety-word mini-stories about what this person would do in these situations. In each the person's personality sets the action in motion. Your person . . .

1. accepts the wrong job.

2. is wrongly accused of a crime.

3. falls in love with a brother's or sister's spouse.

4. takes up photography.

5. runs for political office.

6. loses his or her nerve.

7. joins a secret society.

OR: Come up with your own idea for a mini-story.

 Write Away!

1. Pick the mini-story you like most and make it more fictional by changing a key element such as a character or the setting.

2. Study your new draft and consider the following: Does your person seem real? What motivates your person? Is there some suspense? Does the setting contribute to the story line?

3. Write the final draft.

 Read and Write

Consider reading "A Christmas Memory" by Truman Capote. Readers of *To Kill a Mockingbird* will recognize a number of similarities between the narrator and the character of Dill. Both are based on Harper Lee's childhood friend, Truman Capote himself.

 On the Screen

Try watching the film *Starman* (rated PG), a science fiction film about an alien who clones and then inhabits the body of a widow's recently deceased husband. Observe the approach the film takes with the classic science fiction theme that aliens may well be more "humane" than humans.

> **Today's Special**
>
> Want to see how another student used this prompt to begin a full story? See "Ring, Ring, Ring" on page 116.

Your Historical Favorite

Bringing a hero to life

☞ **Start**

> *Who are some of your all-time favorite historical figures? Martin Luther King? Elvis Presley? Rosa Parks? Cesar Chavez? Helen Keller? Jackie Robinson? Cleopatra? Do you admire their courage? Their savvy? Their intelligence? Their morality? Choose one you find especially intriguing.*

❓ **Questions**

After reading the prompt above, answer the following questions on another sheet of paper. Use your answers to help you think about your subject.

1. How did you first learn about this person?

2. What caught your attention right away?

3. What new facts have you come across?

4. What do most people your age think of this person?

5. What else would you like to know?

6. Are there any negative views of this person?

7. How is this figure depicted in photographs or artwork?

8. Who would you cast in a film about this individual?

9. What is this person's greatest personal quality?

10. To what extent was this person lucky?

Getting Started

Summarize what you know and what you feel about this historical figure.

 Starting Your Story

Now that you've put together your thoughts and feelings about this person, you should be ready to write a story. Begin by re-creating an actual event that typifies your person's greatness. Pick three of these seven possibilities and write three ninety-word mini-story versions of that event. Write your story . . .

1. as a children's story beginning, "Once upon a time. . . ."

2. as a children's story from the point of view of the hero's pet.

3. in the first person related by your character.

4. in the first person as diary entries.

5. from an acquaintance's point of view.

6. in the third person by someone impressed by this person.

7. in the third person by a skeptic.

OR: Come up with your own idea for a mini-story.

 Write Away!

1. Pick the mini-story you like most and make it longer.

2. Study your new draft and consider the following: Could this story stand on its own if it didn't involve a famous historical figure?

3. Write the final draft.

 Read and Write

Consider reading "An Occurrence at Owl Creek Bridge" by Ambrose Bierce. Notice the influence of Edgar Allan Poe on this eerie tale set in the Civil War—particularly in the ironic twist at the end.

 On the Screen

Watch a period film (*Robin Hood*, rated PG-13; *Gettysburg*, rated PG; *Dances with Wolves*, rated PG-13; or *Patton*, rated PG, etc.) set in a historical era that you find interesting. How accurately is the era portrayed? What sorts of liberties has the screenwriter taken for the sake of a good story?

Meeting a Challenge

Fictionalizing a personal triumph

👉 Start

> *Recall a time that you met a great challenge. This could have happened in school, after school, on a trip, or anywhere else where you spend your time. It could have been a major event or something small and personal. The point is that it took some doing and you did it!*

❓ Questions

After reading the prompt above, answer the following questions on another sheet of paper. Use your answers to help you think about your subject.

1. How old were you? What was important to you at that time in your life?

2. What challenge did you face?

3. Where did the challenge take place?

4. Were others facing the same challenge?

5. What could be gained by meeting the task?

6. What could be lost?

7. How did you feel right before you began?

8. Were you surprised in any way?

9. How did you know you were successful?

10. What happened right after you succeeded?

Getting Started

As briefly as possible, explain what the challenge was and how you met it.

 Starting Your Story

Now take this satisfying memory and fictionalize it. Begin by writing three ninety-word mini-stories. Change as much as you want but retain the details that stick in your memory. Then have one of the following situations occur.

1. A person who wants you to fail plots revenge.

2. You become a hero.

3. Someone accuses you of cheating.

4. This challenge leads to another challenge.

5. Someone from Hollywood hears of your accomplishment and asks you to be in a film.

6. You are asked to repeat the act but fail.

7. Your longtime enemy asks you to be friends.

OR: Come up with your own idea for a mini-story.

 Write Away!

1. Develop your favorite mini-story into a complete short story.

2. Study your new draft and consider the following: Do we know enough about your main character to care whether he/she fails or succeeds?

3. Write the final draft.

 Read and Write

Consider reading "Rules of the Game" by Amy Tan, a story of parental pride gone wrong. Watch how the young girl's chess-playing ability first serves to strengthen but then later to damage her relationship with her proud mother.

 On the Screen

Watch the documentary *Spellbound* (rated G), a true account of the intense world of competitive spelling. Notice how truth can sometimes be more dramatic than fiction.

Life's Not Always Fair

A lesson in living

👉 Start

> *Recall an incident that proves life can be unfair. Maybe you observed the incident or maybe you were actually involved. The point is that what should have happened did not.*

❓ Questions

After reading the prompt above, answer the following questions on another sheet of paper. Use your answers to help you think about your subject.

1. Where and when did this happen?

2. Who were the people involved?

3. What was the occasion?

4. What should have been a fair outcome?

5. What happened instead?

6. How did the victim—who could be you—react?

7. How did others react?

8. What were the immediate consequences?

9. What were the long-range consequences?

10. What similar occurrences have you heard of?

Getting Started

Quickly and completely, report the facts that made up this perplexing incident.

 ## Starting Your Story

Keeping the details of your own, write three mini-stories, each told by a different person. Feel free to add and change details to suit the narrative. Tell this from the point of view of . . .

1. the victim right after the event.

2. the victim, many years later, who considers this to have been an important life lesson.

3. an outraged outsider.

4. an outsider who sees this as "just the way things go in life."

5. an omniscient narrator.

6. someone who benefited from the injustice.

7. a close relative of the victim.

OR: Come up with your own idea for a mini-story.

 ## Write Away!

1. Pick the mini-story you like most and make it longer. Exaggerate the characters. Give the hero more to lose.

2. Study your new draft and consider the following: Is there a lesson to be learned or a theme to be considered within your story?

3. Write the final draft.

 ## Read and Write

Consider reading "The Bass, the River, and Sheila Mant" by W. D. Wetherell. In this story of a first date gone wrong, the protagonist learns a little more about fishing and a lot more about romance.

 ## On the Screen

Try watching the comedy *Miss Firecracker* (rated PG), the story of Carnelle, a small-town woman who has spent her life in the shadow of her glamorous cousin, Elaine. When the time for the annual "Miss Firecracker" beauty contest comes around, Carnelle is determined to win—with or without Elaine's help.

A Fiasco

An account of "One of those days"

👉 **Start**

> *We have all been part of an event that did not turn out as planned.*
> *Recall a time when something went really wrong. This could have*
> *occurred at a botched wedding, first date, try-out, English test, or job*
> *interview. What was intended to happen did not happen.*

❓ **Questions**

After reading the prompt above, answer the following questions on another sheet of paper.
Use your answers to help you think about your subject.

1. What was the event?

2. Were you a participant or an observer?

3. What was supposed to happen?

4. When did you first sense that things were not working?

5. How did things really break down?

6. What were you doing through all of this?

7. Who suffered the most?

8. In the end was this funny or sad?

9. What future plans were made?

10. Was anyone changed by the experience?

Getting Started

Briefly explain how and why this was such a bizarre occurrence.

 Starting Your Story

Write a short story based loosely on this actual disaster. Begin by writing three ninety-word mini-stories involving disasters in which one of the characters undergoes a change from . . .

1. a bully to a saint.

2. a non-voter to a voter.

3. a follower to a leader.

4. an airhead to a philosopher.

5. a pessimist to an optimist.

6. a policeman to a criminal.

7. a peace-lover to a warmonger.

OR: Come up with your own idea for a mini-story.

 Write Away!

1. Pick the mini-story you like most and develop it into a short story. Remember that you can take this real experience and add further complications to it.

2. Try reading your draft to some friends. Do they find your funny moments actually funny? Do you need more detail to recreate the experience?

3. Write the final draft.

 Read and Write

Consider reading "The Endless Streetcar Ride into the Night" by Jean Shepherd. In this story Ralphie, the hero of the film *A Christmas Story*, is now a teenager and ready to go on his first blind date. Notice how you begin to suspect something's wrong before Ralphie himself figures it out.

 On the Screen

Check out the film *A Christmas Story* (rated PG), which is based on Jean Shepherd's novel *In God We Trust*, a film with a plot made up entirely of scenes that don't quite work out the way people intended.

Fooled by Appearances

When things are not quite what they seem

👉 **Start**

> *Appearances can be deceiving. We have all suffered because we have mistakenly believed what we see on the surface. Recall a time when you were not just fooled, but really fooled by appearances.*

❓ **Questions**

After reading the prompt above, answer the following questions on another sheet of paper. Use your answers to help you think about your subject.

1. How old were you when this happened?

2. What were your favorite activities at this age?

3. What was the occasion for this experience?

4. Where did this take place?

5. What did you think was going on?

6. What was actually going on?

7. How did you make this discovery?

8. What were the immediate results? The long-range results?

9. Did you ever have an experience like this again?

10. When you recall it, what comes to mind first?

Getting Started

Quickly summarize this puzzling event.

 Starting Your Story

Use the plot of this actual experience as the plot of a fictional story. Begin by writing three ninety-word mini-stories for children that begin, "Once upon a time there was . . .

1. a king who thought he knew it all.

2. a raccoon with big ideas.

3. a wizard who owed a lot of money.

4. a naïve piglet.

5. an overly ambitious space alien.

6. a little fellow in a big hurry.

7. an alligator who smiled too much.

OR: Come up with your own idea for a mini-story.

 Write Away!

1. Pick the story you like and expand it. Feel free to add clip art or personal illustrations to the text.

2. Study your new draft and consider the following: Even though your story is intended for children, you will still need to include the basic plot elements (exposition, conflict, climax, etc.) required of any good story.

3. Write the final draft.

 Read and Write

Consider reading "After You, My Dear Alphonse" by Shirley Jackson, author of "The Lottery." In this story a well-meaning mother makes some stereotypical assumptions about her son's new African-American friend. See how the story presents a subtle but strong message about race relations.

 On the Screen

Try renting the film *Roxanne* (rated PG). In this modern adaptation of the play *Cyrano de Bergerac*, the title character must choose between the handsome but obtuse Chris and the witty but homely C.D. Pay particular attention to the scene in which C.D. attempts to feed Chris romantic pick-up lines via a hidden radio transmitter.

Today's Special

Want to see how another student used this prompt to begin a full story? See "Visiting York" on page 118.

Learning Outside of School

A look at the world beyond the classroom

👉 **Start**

> *Consider this quote: "The real lessons of life are learned outside of school." Although you may not totally agree, you must have learned something important outside of the classroom.*

❓ **Questions**

After reading the prompt above, answer the following questions on another sheet of paper. Use your answers to help you think about your subject.

1. What lesson did you learn? Where did this lesson take place?

2. How old were you when this happened? How did you spend most of your time?

3. What didn't you know before this lesson?

4. Were you surprised or did you expect to learn something new?

5. Did you realize at the time that you were learning?

6. When and how did you fully realize that something important had happened?

7. What were the immediate consequences?

8. What were the long-range consequences?

9. Have you passed this lesson on to anyone else?

10. How else could you have learned this lesson?

Getting Started

Explain what this experience taught you.

 Starting Your Story

Keeping this important experience in mind, write three ninety-word mini-stories using your learning experience as the plot. Write . . .

1. an entirely true story.

2. a barely fictionalized true story.

3. a largely fictionalized true story.

4. an animal story for children.

5. a story that takes place during the American Civil War.

6. a myth or legend.

7. a story that begins, "Last week Sam got kicked out of school for good."

OR: Come up with your own idea for a mini-story.

 Write Away!

1. Pick the mini-story you like most and make it longer. Consider changing the point of view from the student to the teacher.

2. Study your new draft and consider the following: Does your story show or tell how you feel? Consider adding irony to contrast what your character expected to learn with what he or she actually did end up learning.

3. Write the final draft.

 Read and Write

Consider reading "Marigolds" by Eugenia Collier. In this coming-of-age story set in the rural South, a poor, young girl takes out her frustration on an innocent victim. Readers of *To Kill a Mockingbird* will notice a strong similarity between the girl's destruction of the old woman's marigolds and Jem Finch's attack on Mrs. Dubose's magnolias.

 On the Screen

Watch the film *Karate Kid* (rated PG), a coming-of-age film set in the world of martial arts competition. Watch how Daniel starts to learn as much about life and respect as he does about kicks and chops.

Loyalty Tested

A detailed account of a magnificent obsession

👉 Start

> *You must know of someone who is fanatically loyal. This person could be loyal to another person, organization, or philosophy. This loyalty is not subtle—it's this person's most conspicuous quality.*

❓ Questions

After reading the prompt above, answer the following questions on another sheet of paper. Use your answers to help you think about your subject.

1. How do you know this person?

2. To what is this person so loyal?

3. What is the cause of this loyalty?

4. How do strangers first notice this loyalty?

5. What would be a good nickname for this person?

6. What major decisions has this person made out of loyalty?

7. What would be this person's worst nightmare?

8. Who might avoid this person?

9. How might this loyalty be tested?

10. Could this loyalty grow into something even more fanatical?

Getting Started

How was your loyalty challenged? Describe the challenge in a few words.

 Starting Your Story

Imagine this person as a character in a story. Begin by writing three ninety-word mini-stories. In each, your person reacts differently to having his loyalty tested. This person . . .

1. remains loyal.

2. remains not so loyal.

3. is no longer loyal at all.

4. changes in subtle ways.

5. becomes even more loyal.

6. says one thing but does something else.

7. goes on to a much better life.

OR: Come up with your own idea for a mini-story.

 Write Away!

1. Pick a mini-story you like most and make the story longer. Consider flashing back to relevant events in your person's earlier life.

2. Study your new draft and consider the following: Does your person's obsession seem real? What motivates this person?

3. Write the final draft.

 Read and Write

Consider reading "Sucker" by Carson McCullers. In this story of friendship and betrayal, the close relationship between two cousins comes to an unsettling ending. Notice how McCullers manipulates the tone throughout the story.

 On the Screen

Try watching the film *Taps* (rated PG). In this film a band of cadets goes to desperate measures to keep their military academy from closing its doors. Take note of the scene in which his fellow cadets honor Brian Moreland after he has been promoted to the rank of Cadet Commander.

Brand-New World

A detailed description of an unfamiliar setting

👉 Start

> *Recall a time when you found yourself in a totally unfamiliar environment. You might have been on a trip to a foreign country or simply in a strange neighborhood. Perhaps this was a return to a familiar spot that had dramatically changed. Maybe you got used to it right away or maybe you continued to be stunned by the changes.*

❓ Questions

After reading the prompt above, answer the following questions on another sheet of paper. Use your answers to help you think about your subject.

1. How old were you at the time?

2. What did you care about at that time in your life?

3. Where was the place?

4. What did you expect to find?

5. What was your initial impression?

6. What were the details that created that impression?

7. How did your reaction to the place change—if at all?

8. How did others react to the place?

9. How did this change you?

10. Have you gone back to that place? How was your visit?

Getting Started

Create an image of this place in a few sentences.

 Starting Your Story

Write a short story with this as the initial setting. Begin by writing three of these opening scenes to begin ninety-word first-person mini-stories. The narrator is . . .

1. looking for a lost love.

2. running from a gang.

3. looking for inspiration.

4. trying to forget a tragedy.

5. suffering from a rare disease.

6. looking for trouble.

7. avoiding a responsibility.

OR: Come up with your own idea for a mini-story.

 Write Away!

1. Pick the mini-story you like most and develop it into a short story. Remember that you can fictionalize this real place to fit the needs of your story.

2. Study your new draft and consider the following: Is there enough sensory detail to create the atmosphere you need for your setting?

3. Write the final draft.

 Read and Write

Consider reading "The Sea Devil" by Robert Gordon. In this story man and manta ray swap roles in an epic struggle for survival both above and below the surface of the sea.

 On the Screen

Watch the film *Doctor Zhivago* (rated PG-13), a story of a gentle Russian poet caught up in the violence of World War I and the Russian Revolution. Pay particular attention to the scene in which Zhivago returns from the war to find that his family's home has been taken over by the government and now houses dozens of destitute families.

Quite a Trip

A journey within and without

☞ **Start**

> *Whether you're traveling across country or just across town, trips produce memories. Make a list of your own vacations or trips. Study the list and then pick the one you enjoy remembering the most. This could have been a totally positive journey or maybe one in which things did not work out so well.*

❓ Questions

After reading the prompt above, answer the following questions on another sheet of paper. Use your answers to help you think about your subject.

1. Where did you go? How were you traveling? For how long? What was the purpose of your trip?

2. How old were you at the time? What mattered to you most?

3. Who traveled with you? Did you all have the same expectations?

4. How well did the trip begin? Was this according to plan?

5. What images can you recall the most vividly from the early parts of the trip?

6. Was there a turning point in the trip? Explain.

7. When were you the most surprised?

8. What was your favorite moment of all? Who was there? What details do you recall?

9. What went wrong on the trip? How did people react to these unexpected events? Did they make a difference?

10. How well did the trip end?

Getting Started

Write a super short narrative of this memorable journey.

 ## Starting Your Story

Fictionalize this trip memory into three ninety-word mini-stories, each of which illustrates a basic truth about life. Here are seven possibilities:

1. We take too much for granted.

2. Life is full of surprises.

3. We can't run away from our troubles.

4. We often astonish ourselves.

5. Out-of-the-way places can be strangely familiar.

6. The farther we get, the closer we get.

7. Little things matter most.

OR: Come up with your own idea for a mini-story.

 ## Write Away!

1. Choose your favorite mini-story and build it into a longer story. Remember, this is fiction so you can add what you want, but don't forget those vivid scenes already stored in your memory bank.

2. Study your new draft and consider the following: Is the added material as believable as the original scenes, or can you tell where the nonfiction leaves off and the fiction begins?

3. Write the final draft.

 ## Read and Write

Consider reading "Honor" by Betty Dahlin, the story of a family's vacation in Ecuador. When a friendly hotel worker steals their money, they must decide what to do.

 ## On the Screen

Watch the film *The Accidental Tourist* (rated PG), based on the novel by Anne Tyler. It tells the story of Macon Leary, a writer of travel books for people who hate to travel. Notice how his uneventful journeys abroad mirror his uneventful journey through life—until he meets Muriel, that is.

A Disagreement

Burying the hatchet

👉 Start

We've all argued with friends. Sometimes these disagreements grow into deep-seated feuds, which can end friendships. Usually, though—especially if the friendship is strong—the quarrel is short-lived. Recall a time when you and a friend quarreled for a short while but finally managed to put the disagreement behind you.

❓ Questions

After reading the prompt above, answer the following questions on another sheet of paper. Use your answers to help you think about your subject.

1. Who is your friend? Why do you like this person so much?

2. What were you doing right before the disagreement started?

3. How did it begin?

4. How did the disagreement affect your relationship?

5. How did others react to what was going on?

6. How bad did the situation get?

7. Did anyone try to help out?

8. How did the disagreement finally end?

9. In retrospect, who seems to have been more at fault—you or your friend?

10. Did your friendship change in any way because of this disagreement?

Getting Started

In no more than twenty-five words, capture the essence of this conflict.

 Starting Your Story

Use this true event as the basis for a fictional story. Begin by writing three ninety-word mini-stories that change the outcomes of the actual events.

1. Instead of ending, the disagreement escalates into violence, affecting the lives of many other people.

2. An outsider tries to help but instead makes matters worse.

3. The disagreement ends, but so does the friendship.

4. The friendship grows much stronger.

5. The disagreement ends, but another, worse one begins.

6. Both people pretend that it's over, but it really isn't.

7. The two friends recall the incident many years later.

OR: Come up with your own idea for a mini-story.

 Write Away!

1. Pick the mini-story that seems the most promising. Spend time showing the friendship before the quarrel.

2. Study your new draft and consider the following: Do the characters have much to lose? Do we care if they reconcile or not? Is the end result too easy?

3. Write the final draft.

 Read and Write

Consider reading "The Southpaw" by Judith Viorst, a story about a girl who wants to pitch for the boy's baseball team and a boy who resists the idea. See how Viorst's decision to write the story entirely in the form of notes passed between the two establishes the characters of the two children.

 On the Screen

Consider watching *The Buddy Holly Story* (rated PG), a "biopic" about the legendary rock 'n' roll pioneer Buddy Holly. Pay particular attention to Holly's relationship with his band, The Crickets, and the poignancy of their failed reconciliation at the end.

Surprising Folks

A look at the truth within

👉 **Start**

> *People do not always live up to their reputations. (Joe is not really a bully. Polly only looks like a bookworm. If Sid smiled more, people wouldn't think he was such a grump.) Recall a time when a person turned out to be not what you expected. You can pick either an obvious or more subtle example.*

❓ **Questions**

After reading the prompt above, answer the following questions on another sheet of paper. Use your answers to help you think about your subject.

1. What was going on in your life when this occurred?

2. Who was the person in question?

3. What was this person's reputation?

4. How did you learn about this reputation?

5. How widespread was this reputation?

6. What was your opinion of this person before you knew the truth?

7. When did you first have a chance to find out what this person was really like?

8. What did you discover?

9. What did you do?

10. What kind of a relationship have you had with this person since then?

Getting Started

Why was this episode so surprising? Explain.

 ## Starting Your Story

Fictionalize your recollection of this discovery. Start by writing three ninety-word mini-stories. In each the discovery has a profound consequence for the person whose true personality is now uncovered. Choose from among the possibilities listed below. The person . . .

1. changes his or her lifestyle.

2. never forgives the person who discovered the truth.

3. changes in subtle ways.

4. tries hard to live up to the false reputation.

5. moves out of town.

6. doesn't quite "get" what happened.

7. runs for political office.

OR: Come up with your own idea for a mini-story.

 ## Write Away!

1. Pick the one you like best and make it into a longer story. Keep the details of the actual event.

2. Study your new draft. Can we see for ourselves that the initial impression was false? Is the aftermath of the discovery believable?

3. Write the final draft.

 ## Read and Write

Consider reading "The Story of an Hour" by Kate Chopin, the story of woman who learns that her husband has been killed in a train accident. Pay particular attention to the irony of the "shocking" ending.

 ## On the Screen

Try the film *My Bodyguard* (rated PG). In this film the new kid, Clifford, attempts to deal with the local bullies by hiring a little "muscle" of his own—a large, brooding boy named Linderman. Notice how their friendship grows as Clifford realizes that Linderman is not the monster he first appears to be.

A Revealing Place

Location, location, location

☛ **Start**

> *Imagine that you are conducting a tour of your neighborhood. Pick a spot—a street corner, an alley, a restaurant, or a park—that is an essential part of your town's personality. To understand this spot is to understand the place where you live.*

? Questions

After reading the prompt above, answer the following questions on another sheet of paper. Use your answers to help you think about your subject.

1. What is the place?

2. What might an outsider say about this place?

3. What are the most obvious features?

4. What are the least obvious features?

5. What are the smells?

6. What are the sounds?

7. What would be out of place in this place?

8. How do you feel about this place?

9. Why might someone hate this place?

10. What would the town lose if this place were removed?

Getting Started

Weave all of your details into a two-sentence description of this place.

 ## Starting Your Story

This would be a good location for a story. Start by writing three ninety-word mini-stories of events that occur in this place. In each, something important happens. You will need to create characters who face problems or issues. Here are your choices:

1. The librarian falls in love with the chief of police.

2. An animal is killed.

3. Someone decides it's time to move far away.

4. The town bully decides to become a priest.

5. A crime is committed.

6. A mystery is solved.

7. A nerd gains some respect.

OR: Come up with your own idea for a mini-story.

 ## Write Away!

1. Pick the mini-story that seems the most promising and develop it. This is your place; make sure that it plays an important part of the story.

2. Study your new draft and consider the following: Can you improve the realism of your place by incorporating real people you know into the story?

3. Write the final draft.

 ## Read and Write

Consider reading "Haircut" by Ring Lardner. Note Lardner's use of irony as the barber/narrator manages to tell his customer a story without fully understanding the situation himself. Try to determine at which point the reader starts to be more aware of what happened.

 ## On the Screen

Treat yourself to the classic film *Casablanca* (not rated), about Rick Blaine, a bitter, expatriated American nightclub owner reluctantly drawn into the fight against the Nazis. See why sooner or later "*everyone* comes to Rick's."

School Days

Going back to the beginning

👉 **Start**

> *Like it or not, you spend a lot of time in school. School has had a profound effect on the person you are becoming. Sit for a moment in a quiet place and go back in your mind to your early school days.*

❓ **Questions**

After reading the prompt above, recall the moments listed below and for each write a short, precise description. What do you remember about . . .

1. climbing on something at the playground?

2. getting mad at a friend?

3. receiving praise from your teacher?

4. eating lunch?

5. making something in art class?

6. losing something?

7. waiting to get picked up at the end of the day?

8. sitting at an all-school assembly?

9. looking out the window?

10. talking to a new kid?

Getting Started

Shape your details into a short-short memory piece about elementary school.

 ## Starting Your Story

With these memories freshly in mind, imagine you are now forty-three years old. Write three ninety-word mini-stories, each a letter to an old classmate from your elementary school days. In each letter you refer to these experiences, but in each you draw a different conclusion. You have now decided that school made you . . .

1. believe in the basic goodness of people.

2. distrust adults.

3. love the outdoors.

4. love learning.

5. become a recluse.

6. become an artist.

7. become a revolutionary.

OR: Come up with your own idea for a mini-story.

 ## Write Away!

1. Pick the mini-story that seems the most promising and expand it into a full story. Remember that, as William Wordsworth said, "the child is the father of the man."

2. Study your new draft and consider the following: Does your narrator view these memories with a mature perspective, or are the memories still too fresh for this person?

3. Write the final draft.

 ## Read and Write

Consider reading "Charles" by Shirley Jackson, a story of a young boy who astounds his mother with tales of Charles, the terror of his school. As the legend of Charles grows, the reader begins to suspect that there may be more to this story than the little boy is letting on.

 ## On the Screen

Try watching the mini-series "Anne of Green Gables" (rated G) about Anne Shirley, a red-haired orphan girl with a fiery temper and a vivid imagination. Notice how the details may have been different back in the nineteenth century, but the personalities still remain pretty much the same today.

Back to School

A look at the "Wonder Years"

👉 **Start**

> *Middle school and high school memories, like elementary school memories, can stir our imaginations. From this wealth of recollections you certainly have the material to write an original short story.*

❓ **Questions**

After reading the prompt above, start by writing down your recollections of these middle school/high school moments. What do you remember about . . .

1. arriving the first day?

2. sitting in a class you do not like?

3. discussing a paper with a teacher?

4. getting in trouble?

5. waiting for the bell to ring?

6. playing basketball in gym class?

7. dancing at the prom?

8. taking a final examination?

9. standing in front of your open locker?

10. eating in the cafeteria?

Getting Started

Tie these details together into an overview of your middle school/high school years.

 ## Starting Your Story

Keeping all of these vivid school memories in mind, imagine yourself as forty-four years old and famous. You are writing a letter to one of your teachers telling that person that you now realize how important these years really were. Begin with three mini-stories. You are . . .

1. a renowned poet.

2. a college professor.

3. a spy.

4. a stunt driver.

5. an advice columnist.

6. an adventurer.

7. an inventor.

OR: Come up with your own idea for a mini-story.

 ## Write Away!

1. Pick the one you like most and make it longer. Remember this is a story in which the narrator comes to realize a truth about life.

2. Study your new draft and consider the following: Does each of your characters have a distinct voice?

3. Write the final draft.

 ## Read and Write

Consider reading "Raymond's Run" by Toni Cade Bambara. Notice how the May Day races turn out to be a turning point in the lives of the kids involved. Notice, too, how Bambara effectively uses dialogue and dialect to bring her characters to life.

 ## On the Screen

Try watching the film *Never Been Kissed* (rated PG-13) about a twenty-five-year-old newspaper reporter who is given the assignment to re-enroll in high school and impersonate a high school student. Notice how the situation allows the reporter to revisit and confront her past.

Favorite Stories

Adding a twist

👉 Start

> Other writers can inspire us to make up our own stories. Maybe they are writers of books that we liked when we were younger. What was your favorite book when you were little? Was it a bedtime story like "The Three Little Pigs"? A tale by Hans Christian Andersen? A modern classic like Goodnight, Moon? It's time for you to revisit this story again.

❓ Questions

After reading the prompt above, answer the following questions on another sheet of paper. Use your answers to help you think about your subject.

1. What was the title?

2. Where did you keep the book?

3. What did the cover look like?

4. How did the story begin?

5. What was suspenseful about the story?

6. How did the story end?

7. What was your favorite part?

8. How was the book illustrated?

9. Why do you think you liked it so much?

10. Where is the book now?

Getting Started

In one long sentence, retell the story of your favorite story.

Starting Your Story

Now that you have revisited one of your all-time favorites, you should be ready to write a newer version. Start by writing three modern ninety-word mini-story versions of this story. The plot should be the same, but the characters and the theme will be more up to date. In each the setting should be different. Use three of the following setting choices:

1. farm

2. school

3. kitchen

4. mansion

5. busy city

6. jungle

7. golf course

OR: Come up with your own idea for a mini-story.

Write Away!

1. Choose the mini-story that seems best and develop it. Play around with the point of view. It is all right to let the reader know that this is a modern version of an old story.

2. Study your new draft and consider the following: Does your story stand on its own merits without the original version?

3. Write the final draft.

Read and Write

Consider reading two modern versions of "The Three Little Pigs": *The True Story of the Three Little Pigs* by Jon Scieszka and *The Three Little Javelinas* by Susan Lowell. Notice how changing the point of view in the former and the setting in the latter affect the story as a whole.

On the Screen

Read a plot summary of the Shakespeare play *The Taming of the Shrew*; then watch the modern adaptation, *Ten Things I Hate About You* (rated PG-13). Decide if you think the film script stands on its own merits.

Lost and Found

A detailed description of a scary situation

👉 **Start**

> *It's no fun to be lost. Recall a time from your distant or recent past*
> *when you suddenly didn't know where you were. In the end you found*
> *your way, but for awhile you were terribly upset.*

❓ **Questions**

After reading the prompt above, answer the following questions on another sheet of paper.
Use your answers to help you think about your subject.

1. How old were you at the time? Were you easily frightened?

2. Where did this happen?

3. Where did you think you were going?

4. When did you first realize you were lost?

5. What was your first reaction?

6. What did you decide to do?

7. How well did this work?

8. Were other people upset by this?

9. How did you finally reach your destination?

10. How did this experience change you?

Getting Started

Including both the physical and emotional features, briefly tell the story of this loss.

Starting Your Story

You have just relived this scary real-life episode; now you can fictionalize it by writing three ninety-word mini-stories designed for children. Choose from these possible beginnings:

1. Johnny was late so he decided to take a short cut through the forest.

2. Mitzy should have been paying more attention to the buildings.

3. Sometimes Elmo was a little too curious.

4. If Edna hadn't chased the butterfly, she would have been home on time.

5. Oscar didn't realize it got dark so early in Alaska.

6. Nelly never could read a map.

7. All these little houses looked the same to Frieda.

OR: Come up with your own idea for a mini-story.

Write Away!

1. Take your favorite and improve it. Remember this will be for little kids. Keep it suspenseful. Try to include some parts of your actual experience.

2. Try reading your new draft aloud. Are there any sections that could be more clearly worded? Would clip art help to enliven your final product?

3. Write the final draft.

Read and Write

Consider reading "The Werewolf" by Frederick Marryat. In this classic horror tale, two young siblings must cope with the growing awareness that their new stepmother is leading a dual existence. Pay particular attention to *how* the author makes us care about the fate of the two children.

On the Screen

Watch the film *Into the Woods* (rated G). In this Stephen Sondheim musical, characters from different familiar fairy tales meet and interact one weekend in the woods. Pay attention to what Sondheim has done to create a story that appeals to both adults and children.

Gossip

Looking at a guilty fascination

👉 Start

> *We all know how viciously appealing gossip can be. Some people are surrounded by gossip while others encounter it only occasionally. What are your thoughts and feelings about the subject of gossip?*

❓ Questions

After reading the prompt above, answer the following questions on another sheet of paper. Use your answers to help you think about your subject.

1. Would you like to be known as "a gossip"?

2. Why do most people fear it so much?

3. Why do we find it so fascinating?

4. Where can you find gossip on the newsstand or television?

5. What run-ins have you had with gossip?

6. What people are most inclined to gossip?

7. Who can be especially wounded by gossip?

8. How would the world be different if gossip were outlawed?

9. If you were a boss, would you fire a gossip?

10. Is there anything good you can say about a gossip?

Getting Started

Using all of your responses, write an extended definition of gossip.

 Starting Your Story

Now that you have considered gossip for awhile, write three ninety-word mini-stories. Start each with an opening sentence about gossip. Choose from these possible beginnings:

1. "He's been seeing Sally," Doris whispered in my ear.

2. Bobby was proud of his "A" grade until he heard the rumors.

3. "Can you keep a secret?" Sam asked in a whisper.

4. Felicia would start shouting if anyone called her a gossip to her face.

5. If people don't stop saying those things about me, I'm going to move away.

6. Rumor has it that Mr. Jenkins got fired from his job in Baltimore.

7. Did you ever wonder why Artis never talks about her past?

OR: Come up with your own idea for a mini-story.

 Write Away!

1. Pick the most promising version and develop it. Even though you may not be starting with a single memory, you should work in as much of your knowledge of gossip as possible.

2. Study your new draft and consider the following: How does the gossip spread? Consider cell phone calls, e-mails, chat rooms, and so on, as means of spreading the rumors quickly.

3. Write the final draft.

 Read and Write

Consider reading "The Alligators" by John Updike, a bittersweet story of a fifth grader's first encounter with the heartbreak of romance. Notice how the teacher's own insecurities help to make a bad situation worse when the class starts to gang up against the new girl, Joan.

 On the Screen

Watch the film *Mean Girls* (rated PG-13), the story of a transfer student whose only educational experience has been being home schooled by her zoologist parents in Africa. Notice how screenwriter Tina Fey of *Saturday Night Live* fame has transported the concept of "survival of the fittest" from the wilds of Africa to the halls of an American high school.

Building a Buddy

Examining the rules of friendship

👉 Start

> *We all have a mental image of what a good friend is supposed to be. We make or lose friends because they do or do not live up to our standards. What has experience taught you about friendship?*

❓ Questions

After reading the prompt above, answer the following questions on another sheet of paper. Use your answers to help you think about your subject.

1. How does a friend differ from an acquaintance?

2. How does an ordinary friend differ from a best friend?

3. What should a friend do if you have a bad idea?

4. When should a friend break a promise?

5. What should a friend do if you make a fool of yourself?

6. Should your teacher be a friend?

7. Can a friend be much older or much younger?

8. Does a friend have to consider you also to be a friend?

9. What do we owe to our friends?

10. When does a friendship end?

Getting Started

In no more than twenty words, write a profile of an ideal friend.

 Starting Your Story

Write three ninety-word mini-stories that reveal your notion of friendship. Here are some possible titles. In each story someone should discover a truth about friendship.

1. "The Secret Friend"

2. "The Not-so-friendly Friend"

3. "A Friend Too Late"

4. "A Friend Too Soon"

5. "The End of a Friend"

6 "My Friend's Limits"

7. "My Friend or My Life"

OR: Come up with your own idea for a mini-story.

 Write Away!

1. Develop the one that works the best. Use as many details from your own life as you like. In fact, this story might be based on an actual experience.

2. Study your new draft and consider the following: Do we see why this person is a friend or must we take your narrator's word for it?

3. Write the final draft.

 Read and Write

Consider reading "The Haunted Boy" by Carson McCullers, a story in which the teenage protagonist must come to terms with his fear regarding his mother's mental stability. Notice how his newfound friend cannot quite make the transition from "friend" to "best friend" status.

 On the Screen

Watch the film *Racing with the Moon* (rated PG), a film about teenage friends soon to be parted by World War II. Although this is a period piece, notice how the concept of friendship remains a universal theme.

Distant Role Model

A close look at a remote influence

👉 Start

> The term "role model" might be a bit overused, but we are often influenced by people we admire. Sometimes, however, these influences can come from unexpected sources. Make a list of your role models; then choose the one you remember most clearly.

❓ Questions

After reading the prompt above, answer the following questions on another sheet of paper. Use your answers to help you think about your subject.

1. Who is this person? Occupation? General reputation?

2. What is your relationship to this person?

3. When did you start regarding this person as a role model?

4. What did this person do in a positive way to get your attention?

5. What else did the person do that impressed you?

6. How did you react to this?

7. Did the person seem aware of this influence on others?

8. Did others see this person in the same way?

9. What is your relationship now?

10. How have you changed because of this person?

Getting Started

What did this person teach you? How did this person do it? Tell the story in a few words.

 Starting Your Story

Look again at what you have just written. Then imagine that this person encounters a huge problem but manages to overcome it through strength of character. Start off with three ninety-word mini-story versions. The person's . . .

1. best friend is kidnapped.

2. job is eliminated.

3. business burns.

4. health begins to fail.

5. values are challenged.

6. child joins a cult.

7. reputation is hurt by a false rumor.

OR: Come up with your own idea for a mini-story.

 Write Away!

1. Pick the mini-story you like most and develop it into a short story. Remember that you can fictionalize this real person to fit the needs of your story.

2. Study your new draft and consider the following: Are the character's positive traits convincing?

3. Write the final draft.

 Read and Write

Consider reading "A Summer's Reading" by Bernard Malamud. In this story an aimless young man struggles to find direction in life. Note the irony of the source of his eventual redemption—the neighborhood alcoholic.

 On the Screen

Enjoy the film *Star Wars Episode V: The Empire Strikes Back* (rated PG). Pay particular attention to the relationship between Luke Skywalker and Yoda, the unexpectedly impressive Jedi Master who teaches Luke, "Do . . . or do not. There is no try."

Farewell

"Parting is such sweet sorrow . . ."

👉 Start

> *Saying good-bye to someone special can be an emotional experience. When was saying good-bye really painful for you? Revisit this moment and see what you can find.*

❓ Questions

After reading the prompt above, answer the following questions on another sheet of paper. Use your answers to help you think about your subject.

1. How old were you at the time? What kind of person were you?

2. Who was the other person? How well did you know this person?

3. How did you get to know this person?

4. What did each of you gain from the other person?

5. What was your happiest memory together?

6. What was the reason for the farewell?

7. Where did it take place?

8. What are some of the details that you can recall most vividly?

9. What did you do immediately afterward?

10. How do you feel now when you recall this farewell?

Getting Started

Why was this such an emotional farewell? Tell the story briefly.

Starting Your Story

Make a fictional story out of this actual farewell. Begin by writing three ninety-word mini-stories. In each, the narrator looks back years later and realizes that although the parting was painful, it taught a valuable lesson. Try to include as many details of the actual event as possible. Choose from these lessons:

1. We must go forward.

2. Things are not as sad as they seem.

3. We can become too attached to others.

4. Emotional pain can be worse than physical pain.

5. Words do not always serve us well.

6. The end can be a beginning.

7. Sad can be funny.

OR: Come up with your own idea for a mini-story.

Write Away!

1. Choose the mini-story that feels right. Make sure we know something about the narrator.

2. Study your new draft and consider the following: Does the setting contribute to the emotional power of the moment?

3. Write the final draft.

Read and Write

Consider reading "The End of Something" by Ernest Hemingway. In this story of a romantic break-up, we're intrigued by what we *don't* know about the situation. For some further insight into the break-up of Nick and Marjorie, read the follow-up story, "The Three-Day Blow," in which Nick discusses his decision with his buddy, Bill.

On the Screen

Watch the science fiction film *Cocoon* (rated PG-13). In this film, senior citizens are offered the opportunity to stay young forever but with a catch—they must leave Earth to do so. Pay particular attention to the mixed emotions the offer stirs in some of the retirees.

Where Do You Go from Here?

Single-Sentence Prompts

Up until this point, you have been responding to very specific prompts. Now you are ready to make more of these choices yourself. Rather than being presented with prompts, questions, and suggestions for your stories, now you will be given a single sentence to use somewhere in your story.

After you have written two or three mini-stories using the lines provided, select one and write a full draft. Then examine your new draft with these questions in mind:

- Have you selected the right point of view? What if someone else were to relate the events?

- Have you made the setting part of the story?

- Are the characters believable? Sufficiently developed? Motivated?

- Does the story start in the right place? Is the conflict clear? Is there suspense? Does the story end where it should?

- Is the theme—if there is one—apparent without being too obvious?

- Is the writing clear and appropriate?

The sentences are listed beginning in the column to the right. Feel free to pull some of your own from stories, novels, newspaper articles, magazine features, movies, song lyrics, and so on.

1. Let me tell you why I burned my money.

2. "Hey look!" a voice echoed through the neighborhood.*

3. Living on a farm year 'round can be hard.†

4. Before I turned out the lights, I checked the locks.

5. Mrs. Spears kept a Confederate flag in the closet right next to her fishing tackle.

6. The car glided across the road and onto the frozen lake.

7. The yuppies are everywhere, but not in my neighborhood!

8. I wasn't tired or bored, but I still decided to yawn.

9. Never underestimate angry grandmothers.

10. Hillary was the first person of color to enroll in our school.

11. Why was Reverend McBride staring so hard at me during his sermon?

Today's Special

Want to see how another student used this prompt to begin a full story?

* See "The Dare" on page 120.

† See "When I Climb into Trees" on page 122.

12. During the Depression, hobos used to come to our back door.

13. I always closed my bedroom door so I wouldn't hear Mother cough.

14. Practice doesn't always make perfect.

15. Sometimes what you see is all that matters.

16. I wasn't pleased when Hugo invited me to the dance.

17. Baby Louie was the best card player in our dorm.

18. Who says little things don't matter?

19. Unless you have to pass through Gibbon City, I would suggest you stay away.

20. Believe me—ghosts do not exist.

21. My uncle never looked me in the eye.

22. Working for Phyllis was no walk in the park.

23. Pigs aren't that stupid.

24. It was a much larger container than I had expected.

25. Did I ever tell you about Telly's game?

26. Up until a few days ago, I had always despised flirts.

27. I ran faster than ever, but the monster was still right there behind me.

28. Tilly collected memories.

29. The old guy cleared his throat and began to speak.

30. Can you believe that I fell asleep during my physics final?

31. I had been ecstatic many times and miserable too, but until Daphne's party I had never been ecstatically miserable.

32. It's never too late.

33. Uncle Cisco loved to annoy his relatives.

34. If you want to learn anything that matters, talk to Old Sally.

35. Maps! I loathe maps!

36. If you think Bruno is stubborn, wait until you meet his twin sister.

37. I always wanted to make movies.

38. Wanda should have trained dolphins.

39. Last night I dreamed a giant chest of drawers chased me down a long, gloomy corridor.

40. Herbie leaned over and kissed me on the forehead.

41. I fell for Mona on our first trip to Jupiter.

42. Was Pedro smirking? I couldn't tell.

43. Everybody thinks that toll booth operators have it so easy.

44. Did you ever fall in love with your past?

45. Life in our family changed big time after Mama took up kick boxing.

46. Who knew that traffic cops could be so touchy?

47. Life's not easy when you look like a movie star.

48. None of us kids wanted to walk by the Miller house.

49. After many years, Mother finally showed me the letter.

50. Amen!

One Final Story

Pick one of your stories and keep improving it. You might go all the way back to Moe's Café, or perhaps you'd prefer to work on a more recent draft. Just make sure that this is a story that you care about.

1. **Reread your story several times and then consider these questions:**

   • What kind of story is this? Coming-of-age? Slice-of-life? Satire? Fantasy?

   • Who's the intended audience? How do you want the audience to react?

   • What are the story's strengths? How could you do even more with these strengths?

   • Do you see anything now that you didn't notice the first time you wrote the story?

2. **Consider some major overhauls. Should you . . .**

   • change the narrator?

   • add a new character?

   • start in the middle and use flashbacks?

   • stress a more apparent theme?

   • create more suspense?

3. **Write a new draft of the story. Then evaluate it by considering these questions:**

   • Point of view: Have you selected the right narrator?

   • Setting: Is the setting well established? Does it add to the story in some way?

   • Plot: Does the story start where it should? Do you provide sufficient background? Is the conflict established early enough? Is it clear? Are there many reasonable outcomes? Is there suspense? Does the story end where it should?

   • Characters: Are the characters sufficiently developed? Are they realistically motivated? Do they push the plot forward? Do the minor characters serve a definite purpose?

   • Theme: Is it clear without being too heavy-handed?

4. **Rewrite it one last time.**

   Then put it away for awhile. No story's really ever done—it will be waiting for you when you're ready to return to it. Besides, there's plenty more where that one came from!

A Stranger's Request

by Ariel Ranieri (age 16)

(See page 42.)

I WAS NOT A PHILANTHROPIST, that was for sure. I wasn't into doing good deeds in order to secure myself a place in Heaven, or wherever.[1] In my opinion, all that mattered in life was luck. Either you had good luck or bad luck, and that was that. Example: one time in kindergarten the ice cream truck came to school, and I was the last one up to the truck, and he'd run out of ice cream. The kid before me was really sorry, and I was kind of a jerk to him. He got food poisoning. Since then, as far as I can remember, I'd been quite lucky. And that's the way I liked it. Why bother with good deeds? I mean, not like I was horrible. I just kept to myself. That was all.

One day at the beach, though, all that changed. I was in a good mood, maybe that's why, or maybe I just honestly changed. Whatever the cause, I altered the way I look at the world, and this was what happened:

I'm an interior designer, and I have my own agency and everything, MacKensie Thompson Design, Ltd. I remember I was on vacation in Hawaii that day, because a client and friend I worked with gave me tickets she wasn't going to use. So there I was, not a thing to do for a week and loving it.[2] Sunning myself into oblivion. And then:

"Excuse me, could you just keep an eye on my daughter for a few minutes? I left something in the car, and it's such a hassle to bring her along." The speaker was a shortish woman with big glasses and blonde hair that looked fake. She had sand on her neck, but I don't know if she knew.

I was rather taken aback. In fact, so taken aback that I said, "Yeah, sure," before I'd even had time to think.

"Oh, thank you so much. She's just right over there, in the blue bathing suit. Just make sure she doesn't go in the water, alright?" And then she was hurrying away, keys jangling in her hand.

I turned to look at the girl. How easy would it be for me to walk over, put her in my car, and disappear forever? I mean, if I had any reason to, which I didn't. I hated kids, actually. And money from ransom? I had plenty of that. But supposing it hadn't been me the woman came to. Supposing it had been a kidnapper?[3]

Suddenly the girl looked up and saw me watching her, tilted her head and stared at me for a moment, then got up and came over. "You're watching me."

"Yes, until Mommy gets back."

I've said I didn't like kids, but actually this girl interested me. She had this quiet, mature look on her face, like she saw and understood more than anyone could imagine. And she was quiet. Soft-spoken. Calm. "Mommy's not coming back, actually. She's not really my mommy."

"Oh, I see." I supposed it was some sort of childish game. Maybe she wasn't any different after all.

"You don't believe me, of course. Adults never do. I'm just a silly little girl." She shrugged, as if she didn't really care. "Mommy's not coming back." She turned away and walked calmly back to the same spot where she'd been digging aimlessly deeper and deeper.

I felt kind of bad for her. She obviously believed the story herself, which was sad. So I got up and sat down next to her. "Where are you digging?"

"They say if you dig long enough, you'll reach China." She cast her little plastic yellow sand shovel aside and began digging with her hands again. "I don't believe them, so I'm out to prove them wrong."

"Well, theoretically you could, but it would take a long, long time like that, and it gets really hot in the middle."[4]

"Oh." She paused. "So I couldn't."

"Not like that, no. Not unless you had a long, long time and a special suit so you wouldn't melt." I hesitated. "Or implode."

"Implode?"

"Get crushed."

"Oh."

"So why do you say Mommy's not coming back?" I craned my neck to see the beach entrance, but the woman wasn't back yet.

"Mommy's dead. So's Daddy. That woman is Aunt Sylvia. But she doesn't like me. She wants to get rid of me."

"That's a bit harsh!" I said with a laugh. "Are you sure about that?"

She gazed up at me. "I heard her say it to her cat. She didn't think I was there. She didn't see me, either."

I frowned. "Are you sure she wasn't just joking?"

She focused back on the sand castle and shook her head. "She was serious."

I realized now what position I'd been put in: I could no more leave the girl here than take her with me. On the one hand, I wasn't sure I wanted that responsibility. But on the other hand, I couldn't just leave her here. That was cruel. She'd just continue digging, trying to reach China, waiting for someone to find her and take her home, and eventually die of thirst. But then again, if the aunt were charged with abandoning her daughter, she could turn it around and say I'd kidnapped the girl. So what was I going to do? Just leaving the girl there was morally unacceptable.[5]

I smiled quietly, wondering where all that moral stuff had come from. And yet . . . leaving the child there alone was something I knew I couldn't do. And it wasn't because I was afraid of being punished, or I would feel guilty, or anything like that. It wasn't a selfish thing. It was just that a child like that deserved to live. "I'll tell you what," I said at last. "If Aunt Sylvia doesn't come back, I'll make sure you find a home."

She nodded, and the conversation died, and I got up and went back to my towel. Four o'clock passed, and so did four thirty, and five, and five thirty, and then six and seven. Finally, at seven

thirty, I'd had enough. It was getting late, and I was getting hungry.

"Does your aunt have a cell phone number?" I asked when I'd gathered up my stuff and walked back over to the girl.

"Yes, but she won't answer it."

"All the same. . . ." I dialed the number she told me and waited. It rang, which meant it was on, but no one picked up.

"Your call has been forwarded to an automatic voice message system. The number you called is not available." And then came the beep.

"Hi, this is MacKensie Thompson, the woman from the beach, and we're kind of wondering where you are. Anyway, I'm staying in suite 216 at the hotel until the fifteenth, and then I'll be back at my office in Chicago." I left her my cell phone, office, and home numbers and addresses, just to be certain. I'd also taken an extra precaution. I'd copied the message to my phone. I'd send the same one every night. I would not be held responsible for this.

Aunt Sylvia didn't call back that day, or the next, or the next, or the day after. She didn't call back when I left her a message to tell her I was home, and I took the girl, whose name was Heather, as it turned out, to the police station to ask what I should do. They took her from me and put her in a foster center for the time being, but said I could visit her when I wanted to.[6]

"Is it possible that if this woman comes back and accuses me of kidnapping, there will even be a case?" I was too curious not to ask.

The police officer sighed. I liked him, he was nice. "Of course she'll be able to accuse you, if she wants to. And she could theoretically form a case, if she wanted to. But it would be pretty weak."

"I've left messages on her cell phone every night since it happened. If she's deleted them, is there any way to access them, to prove I did?"

"I'm not sure about that. You'd have to talk to the cell phone company. But if you say that, and your attorney asks her that on the stand, she'll have to tell the truth. And I bet there's a way to check messages. It was an honest try on your behalf. I'd say if anyone has a good case, it's you."

"All right." I left feeling slightly less worried.

In time everything played out in due course. It always ends up all right, for me. That's how life works: some are lucky and some are not. However, I've revised my outlook just a touch: good deeds still won't be rewarded and bad deeds won't necessarily be punished, but I've decided a good deed every once in a while can't hurt.

I suddenly am incredibly aware of how selfish people are: they're perfectly fine with donating to charity, as long as they get something out of the deal. Apparently inner peace isn't enough for them. They need material gratification. But I don't.[7]

Now Heather lives with me, and Aunt Sylvia sends a thousand dollars a month to pay for her, as was agreed in court. She is permitted to visit but only for a short time and under my supervision.[8] So far she's stayed away. And that's perfectly fine with me.

At the moment I'm writing this, Heather is at the computer. She's found a new way to dig to China: the Internet. She's proved to be as intelligent and thoughtful as she looked at first glance, and she's a quiet, unspoiled girl who's perfectly capable of taking care of herself, which is helpful because I'm busy a lot.

So in the end, we can conclude thus: I'm just a lucky person.[9]

Notes to the Author

- **Point of View:** The use of first-person was a wise choice because the story is really about the narrator's change in perspective. You maintain a believable voice throughout the story. You also create the chance that she's not quite as hard-boiled as she at first sounds.

- **Setting:** You could do a little more here. How about a panoramic view of the beach? The sound of the waves, the smell of the suntan lotion, the zinc oxide on the lifeguard's nose . . . .

- **Character:** Both the narrator and the little girl are well developed: We understand their actions and reactions. The aunt remains a mystery, but that may be an effective plot device.

- **Plot:** Your dialogue advances the story well. We see the problem right away: Will the experience with the child change MacKensie's world view? While it's not overtly suspenseful, it is possible that the woman might return and reclaim the child leaving MacKensie just as cynical as she was before.

- **Theme:** You need to find a new way to express the theme. Instead of stating the theme outright, let the characters' actions speak for themselves. In this case, that should be enough.

- **Now What?** You write excellent dialogue. In your future stories, continue to have your characters talk a lot.

Comments

1. Good start—tells us a lot about the character and gets the action moving.

2. Effective background information—it gives us a sense of who she is and why she's there.

3. This internal dialogue works.

4. This sounds like real talk—something many writers struggle to accomplish.

5. Your narrator starts to change her outlook subtly—good foreshadowing.

6. This seems too easy. Try adding a separation scene here.

7. This moralizing needs to be more subtle and less preachy.

8. You are right to keep this short. Sylvia's personality is not key to this story.

9. Nice play on the concept of "luck."

Hey, Tom

by Dan Kiefer (age 18)
(See page 4.)

HEY, TOM,

So last week I was headed out to visit my aunt.[1] It had been a long day, and I had not eaten since breakfast, so I decide that I would stop at the first place I saw that was open. Not a minute after I had made my decision, I came upon this small place with a faded sign that said "Moe's Café," and I thought I would check it out, even if it was a little rundown. I had no idea what I was walking into.

As I entered, I was greeted by a three-legged dog in great need of a bath. His short rusty red hair was covered in grease stains, and he introduced himself to me with great enthusiasm by putting his front paw on my chest. From across the diner, a chubby little waitress yelled "Get off of him, Tripod!"[2] My new mangy acquaintance sulked away as I took a seat in one of the many empty booths, where I decided I would face the door, just so there were no surprises.

The chubby little waitress approached (Blanche, according to her faded nametag) and asked if I wanted anything to drink as she handed me a menu. She had short, curly hair, an unwelcoming face, and fat bulging from everywhere. From her shoes up, she seemed to have forced herself into an unnecessarily small uniform, which I could only guess had fit her in a previous decade. I wondered if she was able to change, or if she wore everything like a ring you can't get off your finger.[3] Her bulging arms and fingers handed me a menu, which had a limited selection of a hamburger or meatloaf surprise. I said I wanted the hamburger, and Blanche went to the kitchen to put in my order.

I looked around the poorly lit café, first noticing the untidy linoleum floor. In the parts with no linoleum, I could see the exposed dirt floor. The walls were covered in either flowery pink wallpaper that seemed to match Blanche's outfit or olive green pants, depending on where you looked. I could only assume that the redecorating process had been abandoned in the late '60s, leaving the interior in its present state.

In the booth across from my own, there was a family with four boys, only two of whom had shirts. It was nice to see that all six, mom included, had similar taste in hair, for they all had nearly identical mullets. Behind the counter, I noticed for the first time, in all his glory, Moe himself. He was a tall greasy man in a sweat-stained t-shirt, with his slicked-back hair kept in a hairnet. He gave me a smile, exposing his missing and gold teeth.[4]

Blanche came with my hamburger, which seemed to have been prepared a week or two before. The bun was stale and moldy, and the burger was burned to a crisp, but was only room temperature. As I examined the burger, I finally came to the conclusion that this was in fact the worst dump I had ever been in, and given my sizable experience in eating in dumps, this was quite a statement.

As I marveled at the incredible dumptitude[5] of my surroundings, something caught my attention from across the room. I turned to see the most beautiful girl I had ever seen, and given my sizeable experience with beautiful girls, this is quite a statement. She was modestly dressed in jeans and a t-shirt, her hair was pulled back, showing her un-made-up face, which did not require any makeup to enhance its look.

I sat transfixed. As I stared, she got up from her table and headed for the door. She slowed and said something to Moe, then continued forward. As she walked, she turned, looked at me, and gave me a coy smile. Before I could react, she was out the door.[6] I had the sensation I had just been hit in the chest with a baseball bat. I moved slowly out of my booth toward Moe.

"Who was that?" I asked in a quiet, but determined voice.

"That was my daughter, Margaret."

"Oh . . . ," I said in a stunned voice.

Without thinking, I slowly left Moe's Café. I moved like a zombie to the door, whereupon exiting I searched in vain for my newly discovered hope, but to no avail. She was gone.

I left without paying, and was later stopped by the police and taken into the station where I had to pay a fine. This was the worst and best restaurant I had ever been to, but I can never return, because it seems that Moe has filed a restraining order against me.[7] Aw well I guess. Maybe you should stop by and check out what's going on at Moe's. . . .

Talk to you later, guy.

Notes to the Author

- **Point of View:** The "letter voice" works. It has a conversational tone. We immediately identify with the writer.

- **Setting:** Your choice of detail not only helps us to visualize what's happening, it gives us a sense of your narrator's personality as well. Perhaps you could tap into some of the other senses as well. What did this place smell like? Sound like?

- **Character:** Overall you have created a very believable, motivated human being. We know what your narrator wants and why he wants it. His personality helps to move the story along.

- **Plot:** Your plot really kicks in when he spots the beautiful girl. Now you have raised questions that need to be resolved: Did the girl *really* send him a coy look? Will they get together? Expanding the plot would make it a better story. For example, you could include the scene at the police station.

- **Theme:** There's nothing overt here, but does this tell us a little about human nature? Love is powerful medicine? The world is full of surprises?

- **Now What?** Why not write a follow-up story? Maybe the narrator and the girl could meet again. Maybe he gets an unexpected call from Moe. Maybe he completely misunderstood her look.

Comments

1. Very believable—We can tell right away that he and Tom know each other pretty well.

2. Clever way to incorporate dialogue—great name, too.

3. Fresh simile

4. Effective use of detail

5. Words like this tell us a little about the character himself—he's a word guy!

6. Plot opportunity—is he sure that she's interested?

7. Too fast! This could be broken down into a series of scenes.

Electricity

by Carlos Angelos (age 17)
(See page 8.)

THURSDAYS WERE HOLY TO MY family. It was a routine now: Pack the Gatorades in the fridge for slightly over an hour, not too much or they'd be boulders. Wash Jaime's Nikes with the Penguin bottle polish and stuff them sideways into the duffel bag, being careful not to wrinkle the Heyworth Hornet All-Americans jersey. Last but most important, Jaime always wore his green and gold Notre Dame boxers, so it was up to me to pull them out of the dryer and hand him them steamed.[1] Thursdays were home games at Heyworth High. It's been like this for about six months now, and the phone calls from basketball powerhouses like Michigan State to St. John's are becoming more frequent. I never figured how or why my little brother became the star that he is. He's a high honor student, has a likable character, and is blessed with good looks. But basketball?

Six months ago, Jaime first set foot in Heyworth High School. I, being the older brother and senior, had the responsibility to show him around. He always had his way with academics and sports in middle school. But I figured he would have a wake-up call[2] at a high school that ranked high in both academics and sports. But early on, he showed his talent in the classroom and on the court as a member of the freshman team. Against our crosstown rivals, the Pekin Dragons, Jaime managed to fracture his kneecap on a rebound in the first quarter.

He continued to play and performed amazingly, even with the injury, and led his team into overtime. But the Dragons overpowered the smaller Hornets and took away the win. Since then, Jaime was brought up to the Varsity Team and it didn't take long for him to start as the point guard.

This Thursday was just like any other Thursday. Pack Gatorades, shine Nikes, and steam-press Notre Dame boxers was becoming a ritual to me.[3] This game marked the first play-off of the season for the Hornets, and what better way to begin the post-season than against the Pekin Dragons. Chester, the security guard, greeted us at the door with a grin and waved us into the arena. We sat down at our usual location, which was in the middle of the B section.[4] We arrived twenty minutes early as planned, enough time for Jaime to speak to some of the local press and suit up for warm-ups. It didn't take long for the Pekin Dragons to appear from the locker rooms dressed in metallic green, sporting headbands, wristbands, all sorts of elastic gimmicks that made their players seem bulkier than our players in our white and red jerseys.

The ref blew his whistle, threw up the jump ball, and the game began. We held the lead for the first minutes of the game but the constant pounding of the massive-bodied Dragons seemed too much for the Hornets. At the end of the half, The Dragons held a secure lead. The Hornet fans wondered where Jaime's leadership had gone.[5]

For the first time in the entire season, Jaime was benched for the start of the second half.[6] The Coach for the Hornets was Mr. Screen, a young lad[7] in his twenties dressed in a shirt and tie and carrying some extra baggage around his waist. His neck would turn red at first but then blue if you repeatedly missed lay-ups or free throws. Jaime, in anger, took a seat on the bench while the second half began. The Hornets had some catching up to do, but Mr. Screen's new strategy only made things worse and the gap between the two teams grew. My parents became more outraged with every minute.

Toward the last few minutes of the third quarter, Mr. Screen realized his team needed some sort of direction to finish the game with some decency. He called Jaime to the side and whispered something to his ear. Jaime reentered the game, and it seemed as though the entire pace of the game shifted. The crowd chanted louder and longer and the metallic jerseys of the visitors seemed to fade with every turnover and every Hornet possession. Every lay-up, drive, and jumper was assisted by Jaime. The crowd was fanatical for the unforeseen gain in points and the Dragons began to lose their confidence.

With the score finally tied at 63, The Pekin guard held on to the ball and with a few seconds remaining, took a wild shot. It went in, giving them a lead by two.

All was silent. The cheerleaders stopped flapping their pom pons in the air. The entire crowd, the sky, and atmosphere held their breath. Chester squeezed his arms together, making his pupils brighten and enlarge. Jaime dribbled the ball downcourt with eight seconds remaining with a two-point deficit. I looked over at my

parents and they seemed to have complete faith in Jaime's actions.

I felt my chest tighten and for a few seconds I was drowned out by my own heartbeat. The Dragon players scrambled to Jaime and forced him to pass to his guard Alex. Alex fired the ball back to Jaime, who took the final shot, a three pointer. It hit the rim, rolled around, and went in. We won by a point! I collapsed in my own arms and stayed that way[8] until the lady next to me tugged at my sweater and nodded to the floor, where the fans were all over.

The two teams, in awe, shook hands. Jaime went on to Notre Dame, where he starred on the court. I became a professor and never went to another game. I had better things to do.

Notes to the Author

- **Point of View:** This is obviously very important. You have given the narrator a somewhat "nerdy," distant voice. We know what he likes to do on game day. We know how he reacts to his brother's heroics. This is a big brother's story.

- **Setting:** Because this is the big brother's story, we know as much about the family home as we do the gym. Still you could have provided more details about the gym. What would he have noticed? What are the sights, sounds, and smells?

- **Character:** We know the narrator. We have no way of knowing too much about Jaime—except that he is successful. Is there a way you could sneak more of his character in? Perhaps he has qualities that we can see but the narrator cannot. Maybe he doesn't appreciate his brother's help. Maybe all of this hero worship is starting to inflate his ego.

- **Plot:** You begin early by setting up the family. You build to the climax. The ending is quick, but in keeping with the characters.

- **Theme:** You were not trying to make an obvious point about human values, but you do show that people have different values.

- **Now What?** A follow-up story might be interesting. This could be part of a family saga. What does success do to Jaime? When does the narrator decide to stop going to games? What about the coach? He is unusually young for the job and doesn't seem that sharp. Is there a story there?

Comments

1. This ritual really works to set the situation, especially having to steam his brother's boxers.
2. Great word choice! You are revealing the fussy adult nature of the narrator.
3. This repetition is effective. It really reminds us that this is more than just an action story.
4. The fact that the older brother sits with his family rather than with his buddies further establishes his character.
5. We could use a little more detail on the game and the place here.
6. Slow down and show the crowd reacting to this benching.
7. This unlikely choice of words further establishes the narrator's "adult" viewpoint.
8. Powerful image—foreshadows the ending.

Evanescence

by Mahesh Vallath (age 12)

(See page 34.)

REECE JOHNSON WOKE UP NOT knowing what the date was. Nothing really unusual about that, he reasoned. But it unnerved him nevertheless. He had been diagnosed with possible Alzheimer's disease nearly three years ago. Or was it four? He stowed away these doubts, got up without waking his wife, and quickly made it to work.[1]

Professor Reece Johnson was a tall, stately man getting on in years.[2] His shoulders were stooped, but he was still an imposing figure. He was white-haired, but his moustache was black and his eyes even more so. They had a penetrating quality about them, which was about as malevolent as he would ever get. He had been married to his wife for nearly forty years. He had been a teacher even then. He had once been considered an excellent educator, but he felt he was slipping these days. . . .

His class today seemed restless. Some were eager to start the lesson, while others looked half-asleep. Today's lecture was on the works of Prof. Johnson's favorite playwright, William Shakespeare.[3] Smiling at his class, he motioned for them to sit up and pay attention. He was about to start talking when he paused. Glancing at his notes, he realized he could not make sense of them. . . .

He looked at his class with panic in his eyes, staring at the faces of people whom he had known for nearly a year, yet did not know at all. They stared back at him uncomprehendingly. Distraught, he rushed from the room. Most of the students were upset, wondering what had befallen the professor.[4] They had been looking forward to his lecture. Others snickered. Crazy Johnson was acting up again.

Prof. Johnson got off work early that day. His wife was surprised. "What happened today, Reece? You're not supposed to be home for another five hours," she said. He did not answer. "Do you want something to eat, honey?"[5] He still did not answer. He looked at her with a blank look in his eyes. He had forgotten her. She turned away from him and cried. And there he stood, the look not leaving his eyes. . . .

He sat in a corner, on his favorite chair. His sobbing wife did not approach him. She knew there was no hope. She was only a few feet away, but just might as well have been on another continent. He could not remember her, though he had periods where he was nearly lucid. His memory flickered on and off. He mumbled incoherently, never moving from his spot on the chair. His once penetrating eyes were blank and wide, staring into empty space.

The next day, however, he had regained much of his memory. His wife was still shaken. After reassuring her, he left warily for work.[6] His class was good, and his students had mostly forgotten about the previous day's incident. He assured them that he had just "not been feeling well," Only his wife knew the truth of his condition. Prof. Johnson had put it off as just a possibility, but now, when he had forgotten the names of his favorite authors, and even the name of his wife of forty years, he was sure. It was more than just a possibility.

He still could look forward to the weekend. His favorite student was coming to visit him. He had inspired her to become a teacher nearly thirty years ago, and now she was a full-fledged English professor.[7]

Ever since she got out of high school, they had corresponded regularly. They would debate endlessly about different plays and meet once a year to go to the Stratford Shakespeare festival in Ontario.[8] They would consider everything, and contemplate together possible outcomes if, say, a character behaved differently, or the effects of a subtle change in plot. Those were happy times. But this time would probably be the last.

She arrived and they prepared to leave. But before they left, Prof. Johnson's wife quietly informed her of his condition. The student was upset, but they were still resolved to go. This had been a tradition for nearly twenty years.

The festival, they agreed, was the best to which they had ever been. They saw performances of *Hamlet, Romeo and Juliet, Macbeth,* and many other classics. On the way back, they amused themselves by discussing the actors, the plays, and everything else. They laughed a great deal. They were lost in their shared love of literature.[9]

As they were turning the corner to his home, she noticed something. . . . Reece's once expressive, penetrating eyes were blank. The student inquired,

"What's the matter?" He did not answer. She paused and waved a tremulous hand before his pale face. He still did not respond. She turned away, not wanting him to see her tears. And as she got into her car, he again remembered. . . . He tried to hold her hand again, but she was already gone with the wind.

One year later, he was institutionalized. His wife had been unable to care for him any longer. And there he stayed until the day he died, one year later.[10]

One sunny afternoon in the cemetery, the young English professor came to the grave of Reece Johnson. A tear dampened the ground beneath her feet. She stood there for a minute, memories of old times fading like her tears, and then turned away.

Notes to the Author

- **Point of View:** Using the third-person limited voice was a good choice: We have distance, but we're still inside the mind that matters the most.

- **Setting:** The scenes feel a little bare. We'd like to know a little more about Reece's house, classroom, and the festival.

- **Character:** We need more background on Reece's character. Find some way to *show* some of the ways he had been a great teacher and how he had been slipping. Consider using flashbacks. The wife seems to be an important character. How does she feel about her husband going to the festival with a younger woman? You have done a better job with the younger woman—she is believably motivated.

- **Plot:** This starts and ends well. Although there is an inevitability to Reece's fate, we still find his "small victory" satisfying.

- **Theme:** You succeed in giving this story a universal feeling. Without being too obvious or melodramatic, you dramatize the power of love and the consequences of aging. Those are sophisticated concepts.

- **Now What?** Overall you need to get closer to the action. At times it reads like a plot summary. What if you tried this as a play?

Comments

1. Let us see his bedroom.
2. Good, no-nonsense description
3. Smooth piece of foreshadowing
4. A bit stilted
5. Reminiscent of *Death of a Salesman*
6. Show this scene! Add detail and dialogue.
7. This is a bit rushed.
8. Flashback opportunity
9. How does his wife feel about this?
10. You were right to keep this part short.

Ring, Ring, Ring

by Jesse Welch (age 15)

(See page 60.)

"GOOD MORNING MR. ALARM CLOCK, and welcome to another perfect day in another perfect world!"[1]

Here rises a man, just another man of the world. He wakes up, covers his lion's mane of hair with a cap straight out of the 1920s, and tosses on a coat that looks like he may have just stolen it from a bum. This perfectly normal man throws his 5 foot 1 inch frame out the door for another boring day of his perfectly boring life.

Pirouetting down the sidewalk to a beat only he can hear, he pauses for a moment to inquire of a squirrel the day's weather. He somersaults into the street, leaping high as cars slide to a halt mere inches from his body, the world holding back so he can continue on his blessedly normal life. Screeching tires, screaming drivers, all fall upon ears long since deafened by a lifetime of yelling, and his reverie continues unfalteringly onward.[2]

Bouncing his way onto a train platform to go wherever such a man as this goes to make a living, he sees his friend the squirrel sitting on the tracks. A short leap later and he finds himself beside this strange animal, questioning of it the wisdom of choosing such a place to sit.

The oncoming train slows as much it can, but cannot stop before the impending impact. The man watches the squirrel dive off the tracks and totters after his miniscule friend, pondering why it chose to desert him. The conductor's horn goes unheard by the ears of this man, and the sparks from the wheels unseen. He nearly makes it out of danger following his friend, but in an instant this man's perfectly normal life is away from him in rolling rivers of red.

The flashing orange lights bring his redemption. Doctor's white gloves sew cuts shut with blue thread, as red trapped in body brings pink to man's cheeks, white fog steaming doctor's glasses as white light returns to healing body and white casts are plastered on broken legs.

The man wakes up in his home, released after weeks by the hospital to become, again, just another man of the world. He wakes up, and reaches for a 1920s cap, stolen while he was unconscious, to cover a mane of hair shorn off so doctors could place stitches. The corner of his eye glints in the morning sun, and the colorless water welling flows down his cheek, far more painfully than the red that once did.

He reaches for the coat that was rescued along with his body, and finds it as battered as himself. Throwing its tattered remains aside, he crawls into the wheelchair that will replace his legs as far forward as his clouded mind can see. He slowly rolls out his front door and down the board placed upon his step, the best ramp he can afford to buy.[3]

Rolling slowly down the street, cursing the world, the man comes upon a squirrel, eager to converse again about the weather. His body surging with anger, his usual kind words are replaced by angry shouts, as the animal scurries away in fear. Realizing what he has done, he cries out an apology, begging his friend to return to him. The agony in his eyes abates as the small furry creature slowly edges back, and they have a perfectly normal conversation on this perfectly normal day.

The man rolls away, and turns in a slow circle, a shadow pirouette, as the music within him starts again, and he dances through life to a beat only he can hear.[4]

Notes to the Author

- **Point of View:** Your decision to use a "formal" voice has greatly affected the entire story. We are as aware of the *teller* as we are of what is being *told*. This voice enables you to use humor to satirize your main character.

- **Setting:** Although setting doesn't seem to be a key element to this story, you could have used a little more scenic detail. What kind of town is this?

- **Character:** The fact that neither your narrator nor your main character views the man as being unusual makes him seem even more unusual. Your main character's choice to talk to the squirrel sets up the story.

- **Plot:** The question we ask ourselves: Can such a naïve individual survive in the real world? In the end we find out.

- **Theme:** Your choice of voice makes this story read almost like a fable. It shows that eccentric behavior can be risky.

- **Now What?** Have somebody else tell this story. Add a few more characters. Consider having this story be the first chapter in a longer work.

Comments

1. Good, crisp start

2. You really show him in action. Within a few sentences we get a very clear idea of what he is like.

3. Effective use of contrast. We see what his new life will be like.

4. We're pleased that there is a small victory here. It would be a much different story without it.

Visiting York

by Kate Burgoon (age 15)

(See page 70.)

THE INTERNET AND SHOWS such as *Gilmore Girls* hide the irony that comes along with prestigious schools such as Colombia, Brown, and York. When I search for Standish pictures on the Internet, I find a clean campus, lush green quads, and a surrounding town of beauty. Unfortunately, life is not always as pristine and beautiful as the Internet would lead us to believe. If you are lucky, sometimes the truth of the world can open your eyes to the truth of yourself.[1]

I have wanted so bad to go to York. I have flags and pictures on my wall. My screensaver and desktop show pictures of various buildings on York's campus. I know everything about York: average SAT scores, undergraduate and graduate majors, the latest research being conducted. When I was ten, my mom went to visit my godmother (her best friend) who was an administrator at York. When my mom returned, she gave me a York outfit and told me stories about what a good school York was. Since then I have believed that York was the ideal school for me. I would imagine myself standing next to the Woman's Table, eating in the quad, and even reading in the library.

I was ecstatic when my mom told me that we were going to New England. I finally had the opportunity to visit this summer; I counted down the days and thought of how great it was going to be not to have to imagine myself there any more. When the day finally arrived, I couldn't wait to get there; I could hardly contain myself as we drove into the town.[2] When we finally arrived on the campus, my jaw hit the ground, not because of the ivy-covered buildings or beautiful sculptures, but what I saw immediately outside of those gates, the gates that I once thought were the symbol of perfection. I quickly became disillusioned with York, and it saddened me. I was

truly in shock, I wanted so badly to sit down and relax, but I couldn't; there was a homeless person sleeping, living on every bench. I had always imagined York as a place I could feel at home, a welcoming place that could provide comfort to me. Contrary to my visions, there were locks on every single door; police patrolling the campus. I couldn't get in to see the dorms because of security. It disappointed me that there was a world of poverty directly outside York's gates.[3]

While I was visiting the art gallery, I saw a man sitting on a bench outside the Art History department. He struck up a conversation after hearing my comment, "York birds, don't they look smart!" He told me that birds evolved from dinosaurs, and how birds are very intelligent; I assumed he was a student as he continued to elaborate on the topic.[4] As I exited the building a few hours later, I noticed that he was still there. I began to wonder why someone would sit outside a building all day long. That night on the way to dinner, it occurred to me that perhaps he was not a student, and that the bench might be his home. He was there every time we passed for two days; at night we would see him sleeping there. During dinner one night, I had that turning feeling in my stomach, the feeling you get when you are on a roller coaster, or when something isn't right. That man just wanted to talk; he just sat and slept on the bench all day. It was apparent that he was lonely; he didn't want money—he didn't even ask. The longer I sat there, the sicker I felt, so I decided to bring him my dinner. When I approached him with this small gesture, he looked shocked,[5] but he wasn't the only one; bystanders stared at me, perhaps worried that I was in danger. Their faces wore masks of disgust and horror. Some may have found the gesture thoughtful, but most appeared shocked. A moment that should have made me feel better just fueled my anger in regard to the situation. What caused these people to become such harsh judges of another human? How can some people simply ignore another human that is in need?

While some homeless people ask for money, food, or shelter, others crave alcohol, cigarettes, and drugs. To see, firsthand, homeless people living on the streets is truly an eye-opening experience. Worry and anger competed for my attention as I walked these streets, seeing people living in boxes and sleeping on park benches. How can such a rich country still have so much poverty? So many homeless people could use the money that is going to weapons and war. I am

floored that so many people are homeless; I am angry that this country cannot be more successful when addressing ending poverty.

My ideal York is forever changed; today when I think about York I have different visions and different goals. If I do end up at York, I know that my mission will include addressing the overwhelming poverty in the surrounding areas. I chose this lesson because I wanted to go out and help anyone I could after this experience. Maybe someone will want to help when they hear about my experience. This lesson had, and probably will always have, the strongest effect on not only my view of York, but of the world.[6]

Notes to the Author

- **Point of View:** You have created a reliable narrator. She doesn't make excuses for her naiveté, and we can understand why she would feel as she does.

- **Setting:** The setting is a key element to this story. You describe York as a typical Eastern university, while adding enough details to set it apart.

- **Character:** The scene in which your narrator gives her dinner to the homeless man is an important one in establishing her character. Clearly the narrator was expecting him to react a little differently than he did. It would be understandable if at first she was put off by his lack of "gratitude." If her conviction were shallow, that might well be the end of her new commitment. Her commitment has passed the test.

- **Plot:** You find a fresh way to tell the classic coming-of-age story.

- **Theme:** This is a story with a message. You have to be careful not to be too obvious. Let the actions speak for themselves.

- **Now What?** It might be fun to go back and have the mother or the homeless man tell the same story.

Comments

1. Consider omitting this paragraph—let the story speak for itself.
2. Expand this section. Let us see you be impressed first before you become unimpressed.
3. Omit this line—you have already shown this.
4. Let him talk—dialogue would make him seem more real.
5. This is an interesting moment, one worth expanding.
6. This could be a scene with the mother in which your narrator explains her new goal.

The Dare

by Naina Chandan (age 13)
(See page 104.)

HEY LOOK!" A VOICE ECHOED through the neighborhood. "It's the new girl from down the street." I looked from my so-called hiding spot and groaned. It was Tyler Kirk, my next door neighbor, and his posse of idiot friends.[1] Tyler took pride in mocking me and making my life a living nightmare ever since I moved next door.

"Come on, Belly!" he shouted. "It's Belle, smarty." I shot back at him. "OK, Belle," he said grinning as if he had just won the lottery. My immediate thought was something's up because Tyler would never smile like that to me. My next thought was that Tyler wasn't smart enough to think of something by himself, let alone carry it out. "I want you to come trick or treating with us! Our moms already agreed, so don't try to get out of it!" Tyler hollered and ran away while I stared dumbfounded at their disappearing backs.

By this time, you are probably really confused about what's going on, so let me start from the beginning. My mom and I moved to Chicago after their messy divorce because my dad was a drug addict. Everyone knew about my dad back home in Fairfield, Iowa. My friends stopped talking to me and I was left out of everything. My best friend Laura even started to ignore me. Adults looked at me with pity in their eyes. It was almost too much too bear.

My mom told me we were moving to Chicago. I was thinking, why Chicago? What's so good about the Windy City? Secretly I was a little glad so I wouldn't have to endure those pity looks anymore. "Chicago is the place I grew up and our next door neighbors will be my closest friend and her son that's about your age," Mom answered and beamed as if this was the best thing in the entire world.[2]

The day we moved in, Tyler was exactly one day older then me, and his mom came and asked us for dinner at her house. Let me tell you, at the age of thirteen it seems weird for you not to be interested in boys, but that's the way I am. If you took Tyler from another girl's eyes, you might find him to be an attractive guy who is about 5'5" and who has blond hair with green eyes.[3] From my eyes you see an airhead jock who thinks everyone is in love with him. If you looked at me through his eyes, you would probably see an average-looking girl with shoulder-length curly chestnut brown hair. You would also see a new girl who would be fun to annoy.

I ran inside the house as fast as I could, which caused my mother to ask me, "Belle, is everything OK?" I sat down and counted to ten before exploding, "Why did you say I would go trick or treating with Tyler tomorrow?"

"Oh honey, I thought it would be nice if you went with someone your own age instead of with me this year." I knew my mom's intentions were good but she had to pick Tyler to be the person of my age.

"It's OK, mom, I'm going to go change and get ready for dinner." To make it up to me, Mom made tacos, my favorite food.

§

Halloween time arrived and I was going as an angel because I heard Tyler was going as a devil. I thought we should contrast as much as possible. My doorbell had just rung and I was sweating so badly, wondering why in the world they wanted to go with me. The second we were out of my driveway, Tyler said, "I have a dare for you. Don't worry though, it's not too hard. All you have to do is knock on a house of my choice." I look warily at him but just question, "What house?"

"Old Man Jordan's house!" I gasped; that was the house everyone was scared of because it was rumored that if you went there, you got shot. "What's in it for me?" I asked. "I won't ever bug you again," Tyler quickly replied. "Deal," I answered just as quickly.[4]

As we neared Old Man Jordan's house, my hands and body started shaking uncontrollably. Tyler looked a little concerned for me but really excited. I was walking up the stairs when I started to turn back, and to my surprise Tyler was right behind me! "What are you doing here?" I croaked as I struggled to find my voice.

"Do you really think I would let you do this by yourself?" he asked. I looked at him so hard that he squirmed uncomfortably and then I saw him through other girls' eyes, not my own. We had reached Old Man Jordan's house, and before I rang the doorbell I turned to him and said, "If I do this you don't really have to leave me alone." This was my way of telling him that I actually liked him! Tyler's smile was so big that I knew

that he had always liked me. I rang the doorbell and held my breath. An old man answered.

The old man turned out to be Jordan. He said, "Would you like some candy?" Jordan invited us in. We had a great time. We listened to music while Jordan told us scary stories. Jordan told us how the rumor got started when kids started vandalizing his house. He really missed the rest of the kids now that the kids who vandalized his house were behind bars. Tyler and I promised to spread the word about him being a nice guy.

As we were walking home, our bag full of Jordan's candy since he didn't have anyone else to give it to, I realized this was the best Halloween ever. I thought it would be the worst but once again, I was wrong. We neared our driveway and were about to split when I called, "Tyler, come here please." He came and stood there looking curious. I gave him a quick peck on the cheek and quickly walked away. Finally my night was perfect.[5]

Notes to the Author

- **Point of View:** Your narrator tells her story very efficiently. She provides enough background for the story to make sense.

- **Setting:** Because you chose to set your story in a real city, you might as well add a few touches of local color such as deep dish pizza, Cub fans, bungalows, and so on.

- **Character:** You have done an excellent job of making your character a bit edgy at first. Her later transformation is subtle but convincing.

- **Plot:** Your story has definite suspense. Will Belle and Tyler get along, or will they continue to fight? What will happen when they get to Old Man Jordan's house?

- **Theme:** Your story touches upon basic points of human nature (bitterness, acceptance, first impressions) without being preachy.

- **Now What?** Consider expanding the Old Man Jordan character. He reminds us a bit of Mr. Pignati from Paul Zindel's novel, *The Pigman*. Include his scary stories and his explanation of how he acquired such a scary reputation.

Comments

1. Great line—let's see these guys.
2. Short and sweet—a very economical inclusion of background.
3. This is a very clever device: You are able to describe Tyler as being attractive without making your narrator attracted to him. Or is she?
4. Good sharp talk, but you might consider revising this conversation so that each comment is indented.
5. Nice gesture—it shows character change.

When I Climb into Trees

by Jillian Avalon (age 14)

(See page 104.)

LIVING ON A FARM CAN be hard year round. I would rather observe the life around me than live it. My mother always says, "Minty Tadhg,[1] you need to help with the milking, not sit in a tree watching your father work." But I hate milking. I hate farming. It's too confining and I don't get enough opportunity to think. Instead, I will climb into one of our farm's many trees and watch the goings-on around me. I take notes and sketch. I like to think about why things are done the way they are on the farm and what other, more interesting things could be done instead. The farm life is my cage, hoping to keep me locked inside it until all chance of creativity has passed away. I want so badly to be free that to escape this imprisonment, I climb into trees.

One summer day, I woke up before dawn and climbed into a tree facing the fields.[2] I was surprised to find myself shivering with the cold and I was calmed by the quiet. I was the only one awake. There were a few birds beginning to stir and their sweet music filled the air. I watched the horizon as the sky filled with purple and blue. The sunrise painted upward and I could see the purple rise up in the sky, as if God was raising His eyebrow at my being up so early without working. The dew sparkled up to me from the fresh green that is grass. The moon was still lingering in the sky as if waiting to greet the sun. The corn and barley started to sway into a waltz as the wind picked up and I longed to waltz with them.

Then my father stepped out of the house and called out to me. "Minty, help me with the milking, since you're up so early! I could use an extra set of hands!" Alas, to be young and able. I didn't want to be parted from the scene before me, but I knew that to argue would be futile. Father was a stubborn mule when he wished something, and there was no disagreement when it came to work; he was always right. I could hear a "moo" and a loud word which I will not repeat sounding together from the barn.[3] This meant Father forgot to warm his hands, the cow kicked over the milk, or worse still, the cow kicked Father. I reluctantly climbed down for fear of a switching for my sluggishness.

I remember one spring when I was sick, so for once I didn't have to help with the chores. Mother almost didn't let me get out of bed, but I can be as stubborn as Father sometimes and I was desperately missing my time in the trees. I knew that being in a tree would make me feel much better than any stuffy old bed ever would, even if Mother thought otherwise. After all, I would get fresh air! So at noontime I finally persuaded Mother to let me climb into a tree that faced the garden and watched the flowers under a blue and cream sky. The flowers began to dance with the butterflies. I thought of what a lovely view my tree gave me as the world passed on by. The flies and bees shook the pollen into the air causing the noses of my sisters to twitch and sneeze. I laughed at Lavender and Tambre as they played their game of tag through the garden. Their knees were dirty and they laughed as they fell and tripped over each other. I smiled as they picked flowers that they wove about each other's hair. Their voices reached my ears, loud and clear.

"You're it!"

"You're it!"

"You're it!"

"Ouch!"

"You're it!"

"Lavender Delphina! You did that on purpose!"

"Tambre Aine, you know that I very well did not!"

"Yes, you did!"

"Ugh! You're it!"

"Arrrgh! You're it!"

Then I heard the voice of my mother screaming from the porch. "Minty, come inside and eat lunch before you catch your death! I don't want you starving or making yourself worse! And you girls get out of my garden or you'll be weeding the rest of the day!" I climbed down and went inside to eat my lunch, but was very sad. I knew that Tambre and Lavender wouldn't wait for me to finish and I would miss too much for my liking when they moved on to other games.[4]

One winter, my father consented to let me stay up until midnight; after all, it was New Year's Eve and I had finally convinced him I was old enough to handle lack of rest for one night. Sleepily I climbed into a tree facing the house at sunset and watched the sun fade into an ever-darkening sky. The clouds were splattered with oranges and pinks and lined with silver. I could see that the only lighted window was that of my younger brothers' room. They were talking to each other and playing a card game to try and fight off sleep. Howell and Arthur would probably not stay awake until midnight, but they were valiantly waging the war. The window was open just enough for their words to float my way on the icy night breeze.

"Come on Howell, stay awake!"

"It's not all that easy, Arthur. I'm tired and we have to be up early again tomorrow to feed those darned chickens! Besides, Father said not to!"

"Since when did you ever listen to what Father said?"

"Since I started agreeing with what Father said."

"You're no fun. You sound like an old man in the body of a ten-year-old! Go fish!"

"Fine. Got any threes?"

"Go fish."

"How come nobody's been able to say anything but 'go fish'?"

"Because I took all of the matches out of the deck."

"Why the heck did you do that?"

"To keep you talking. That way you'd have to stay awake!"

"Arthur!"[5]

The wind sang a haunting lullaby as I wondered if it was farm life that was making Howell seem old. Life on a farm can suck all the individuality out of people's lives and replace it with the everyday monotony that many people find security in. That is something that I was determined not to let happen to me, so I continued to resist.[6] I would climb into trees and marvel at how beautiful our little farm really was—appreciating it for all it could be and never taking it for granted.

That night I also found myself fighting the daunting sleep. Tiredness washed over me as my watch slowly ticked to midnight and I thought to myself how mesmerizing the stars were. I wrapped my blanket around me and drifted away on the curved branch where I was perched. In the morning I woke to the sound of my father and mother both yelling, "Minty, come inside before you catch your death! You have to eat breakfast and help with the milking!" I slid down the trunk of the tree, frozen like a block of ice. I was glad to go inside to warm up next to the fire—not so glad to milk cows afterward.

As I get older, I find myself sitting in trees less and less. There is more to be done about the farm, and more I can do. Sometimes I can steal away to some tree, if only for moments. Sometimes I still resent the farm work but I realize that it has to be. It allows me to stay in this wonderful place where I've never seen or felt or heard anything quite so beautiful as the sounds, sights, and feelings I experienced in those times of my youth when I climbed into trees.[7]

Notes to the Author

- **Point of View:** Your choice of the first-person limited point of view enables us to understand your narrator's world a little better than she does.

- **Setting:** This is a story about setting. Your ability to recreate the rural world reminds us of Willa Cather's novels. There is a physical as well as an emotional reality here—we know what it feels like to be there.

- **Character:** The narrator is both understandably lonely yet passively defiant: She seems like a real person. Your minor characters serve as effective foils to her change.

- **Plot:** This is more than a slice of life or mood piece. We wonder if she will literally and figuratively come down from the trees.

- **Theme:** Being independent is a mixed blessing. The parents make an interesting choice to let her find her own way even if it takes her away from them. Not all parents would do that.

- **Now What?** This could make for an interesting screenplay. The key would be to let the images speak for themselves.

Comments

1. Consider a different name for your narrator.

2. You could start the story here and work in the details from the previous paragraph along the way.

3. Nice touch—it tells us a lot about her character.

4. This is quite poignant—we feel her affection for the world she can't quite have.

5. You have a good ear for dialogue—it's believable.

6. This really identifies the conflict in the story.

7. This is a rather sophisticated ending—she manages to find a believable way to live in both worlds.